Praise for *Sometimes You Have to Cross When It Says* Don't Walk

"Lesley has been part of the CBS family for more than thirty years and we consider her the trailblazer for women in sports journalism, blessed with both knowledge and heart. Enjoy this romp through her forty years of covering sports."
   —Les Moonves, chairman of the board and CEO of CBS

"I've known Lesley Visser for more than forty years. She covered our team at Boston University for the *Boston Globe*, which was my first head coaching job. Then she served with CBS and covered all seven of my Final Fours. Not much has changed with her from the '70s to now. Lesley has remained charming, talented, witty, and an incredible story teller."
   —Rick Pitino, Hall of Fame basketball coach and winner of two National Championships

"Every single woman writing sports today owes a debt to Lesley Visser, who proved that women could both out-report and out-write men long before we took that for granted, as we do now."
   —John Feinstein, *Washington Post* columnist and bestselling author of more than forty books, including *New York Times* #1 bestseller *Season on the Brink*

"I have known Lesley for decades and she not only loves football, she really knows the game. I recommend this book to anyone who ever wanted to hear great stories from someone who has been around the game for forty years."
   —Dan Marino, NFL Hall of Famer

"Lesley Visser was at Ground Zero for women covering sports, first for the *Boston Globe*, then at CBS. She is one of the greatest storytellers and framers of sports history and many of today's journalists—men and women—stand on her shoulders."
   —Billie Jean King

"Forty years ago, Lesley Visser covered my first professional team, the Boston Lobsters. She earned my trust then and has remained one of my favorite people in sports. Her accomplishments in a male-dominated industry allowed her to break through barriers and blaze a trail that has opened doors for generations of talented women in sports since. Lesley has always been one of the best at getting and telling a story. Now, she tells *her* story."

—Robert Kraft, owner of the five-time World Champion New England Patriots and CEO of the Kraft Group

"Lesley Visser is a giant in women's sports journalism. I don't mean physically, of course. Physically, she has excellent proportions. What I mean is, she blazed the trail for all the women who followed after her. She also paved the way. That's right: This woman blazed AND paved, as well as forging the path, charting the course, raising the bar, and breaking through the glass ceiling. She covered professional football when the gridiron was literally a grid made out of iron and women reporters were not allowed in the locker room without bustles, yet despite these obstacles she broke big story after big story, including the discovery of the forward pass. She was also the first journalist of any gender to spell 'Krzyzewski' correctly. Lesley truly is a pioneer, and all those who followed in her footsteps owe her a debt of gratitude, which they could repay by buying this book. She will also accept cash."

—Dave Barry, Pulitzer Prize–winning author and humorist

"Lesley doesn't demand respect, she commands it."

—Joe Torre, Hall of Fame baseball manager who helped guide the Yankees to four World Series Championships

Sometimes You Have to Cross When It Says *Don't Walk*

A Memoir of Breaking Barriers

LESLEY VISSER

BenBella Books, Inc.
Dallas, TX

BenBella

BenBella Books, Inc.
10440 N. Central Expressway, Suite 800
Dallas, TX 75231
www.benbellabooks.com
Send feedback to feedback@benbellabooks.com

Printed in the United States of America
10 9 8 7 6 5 4 3 2 1

Library of Congress Cataloging-in-Publication Data
Names: Visser, Lesley, 1953—author.
Title: Sometimes you have to cross when it says don't walk : a memoir of breaking barriers / Lesley Visser.
Description: Dallas, TX : BenBella Books, Inc., [2017] | "Distributed by Perseus Distribution"—T.p. verso. | Includes bibliographical references and index.
Identifiers: LCCN 2017030578 (print) | LCCN 2017031608 (ebook) | ISBN 9781944648893 (electronic) | ISBN 9781944648879 (trade cloth : alk. paper) | ISBN 9781944648893 (eBook)
Subjects: LCSH: Visser, Lesley, 1953- | Sportscasters—United States—Biography. | Women sportswriters—United States—Biography.
Classification: LCC GV742.42.V57 (ebook) | LCC GV742.42.V57 A3 2017 (print) | DDC 070.4/49796092 [B]—dc23
LC record available at https://lccn.loc.gov/2017030578

Copyediting by James Fraleigh
Proofreading by Jenny Bridges and Michael Fedison
Text design by Publishers' Design
    and Production Services, Inc.
Text composition by PerfecType, Nashville, TN

Cover photo by David M. Russell
Cover design by Kit Sweeney
Jacket design by Sarah Avinger
Printed by Lake Book Manufacturing

Distributed by Two Rivers Distribution
www.tworiversdistribution.com

To place orders through Two Rivers Distribution:
Tel: (800) 343-4499
Fax: (800) 351-5073
E-mail: pd_orderentry@ingramcontent.com

Special discounts for bulk sales (minimum of 25 copies) are available. Please contact Aida Herrera at aida@benbellabooks.com.

To my husband Bob, my brother Chris, and my
mother Mary, who set wind to my sails when she said,
"Sometimes you have to cross when it says, 'Don't walk.'"

My mother, Mary Visser, with John Madden on the Madden Cruiser
in 1995

PREFACE

People used to ask me where I lived and I'd say, "Baggage claim." It's true. In more than forty years of covering sports, I've been almost everywhere. For ten years with the *Boston Globe*, I covered everything from Wimbledon to the NCAA Tournament, in places like Pullman, Washington; Albuquerque; and two Philadelphias—the City of Brotherly Love, and Philadelphia, Mississippi, where I had to sit outside Marcus Dupree's house for three days hoping I could get a story out of the wayward running back. For CBS, I covered the story of the century, the fall of the Berlin Wall (I broke off small chips to give as Christmas presents), and for ABC I did World Figure Skating in places like London and St. Petersburg, Russia.

Those were trying assignments, and honestly, I didn't see any of them coming. I was just a young girl who loved sports. To imagine that I would ascend to the top of two professions, stay there for forty years, and influence thousands of young women was like saying that I would be the first woman on the Supreme Court (thank you, Sandra Day O'Connor) or the first American woman to go up in space (here's to you, Sally Ride). But I had a true passion for the games; I really cared if the Red Sox moved the runner over or if Sam Jones banked it off the

With Brian Boitano and Peggy Fleming while reporting for ABC at the World Figure Skating Championships

backboard. And I have accepted the scar tissue that has come with being a trailblazer. My husband says if I win one more Pioneer Award, I have to wear a coonskin cap.

I've been able to find humor or pathos in almost all my assignments—I grew up reading Erma Bombeck and Dorothy Parker and the other wits of the Algonquin Round Table (Parker's best line was about when she broke her arm in London "sliding down a barrister"). And through it all, I've had the good fortune to have Barry Frank as my agent, who gave me two pieces of advice: "If it interests you, it will interest the audience" and "Write it down—everything is a bit." This book would be so much easier if I'd listened to the second part. I only took notes for the story I was covering—I didn't want to look like Dustin Hoffman in *All the President's Men*. Remember when someone would say something and he'd run to the men's room, stuff himself in a stall, and write it down on a piece of crumpled paper? I just wanted to live life, not record every second of it.

I always say sports is the great meritocracy. It doesn't matter where your mother went to college or how much money your father has—can you hit the jumper, did you sink the putt? The great Bill Bradley said the mixture of people in a locker room is the "ultimate laboratory." Athletes from every ethnic and socioeconomic background are forced together. This wonderful mix has played out for me, having interviewed five U.S. presidents, every superstar of every color, plus high school quarterbacks, college greats, and kids in slums. I did a terrible infomercial with Marcus Allen (for copper wristbands; it ran at 4 AM and they never sold) and I've been assigned everything from the World Series to *Monday Night Football* to box lacrosse. I've worked with all the great broadcasters and covered almost every sport, and I'm looking forward to sharing the stories and experiences they provided me. I hope you get some inspiration or maybe a few laughs along the way.

CHAPTER 1

How lucky was I to be born in Boston? Boston was interested in three things: the Red Sox, politics, and AM radio, and my family weighed in on all three. We thought the Book of Genesis began with Abner Doubleday. In the late 1950s, it was either WMEX or WBZ. People either listened to Arnie "Woo-Woo" Ginsburg, the leader of *The Night Train Show* on WMEX, or Bruce Bradley on WBZ. I was a Ginsburg guy. He was imaginative, sometimes pretending to be a train whistle or a clown or playing "Does Your Chewing Gum Lose Its Flavour (On the Bedpost Overnight?)." He first played "Louie Louie" as a joke. I even begged my parents to take us to Route 1 North (wherever that was—my family lived on the South Shore of Boston) because some restaurant sold "Ginsburgers." I should actually say I begged my mother, since my father was rarely around.

Max Visser, my father, was born in Amsterdam under the Nazi occupation. My father's father was a doctor, and he went off to Swiss boarding schools and the opera before the Germans came. Even though his family wasn't Jewish, they were all starving for more than five years. Everyone hid a Jewish neighbor, everyone was afraid of the SS. My dad went to Montessori school with Anne

1

Frank. Jews and WASPs all took the same class. When my dad and I would skate on a frozen pond, he would embarrass me by putting one arm low behind his back and a muffler around his neck. He knew nothing of my three passions: football, basketball, and baseball.

My mother, Mary, was the opposite. She was born in western Massachusetts to a poor, funny Irish family. She often told me that if she and Max had dated today, they would have ditched each other in two months. Back then, you got married. She was the first in her family to go to college and she became an English teacher so popular that, at her funeral, more than thirty years of students from her classes came to honor her. She encouraged my love of sports, and told me of the great Wilma Rudolph, who won three gold medals in the 1960 Summer Olympics in Rome. I got to interview Rudolph once, the "Tornado" of Saint Bethlehem, Tennessee, the twentieth of twenty-two siblings. She'd recovered from polio, and I'll never forget how her eyes misted over as she said, "There is no triumph without struggle."

I seldom saw my father because he was a sailor, and a wandering seaman at heart. I was born in Boston but my father sent my mother, my older brother Chris, and me to the Netherlands to live with his mother when I was two years old. Max didn't come, and my mother's Dutch wasn't really that polished, having grown up in the Berkshires. But she looked at it as an adventure (she always said I had "sand in my shoes"), and it must have started my love of travel. My father probably moved three times in the year we lived in the Netherlands. And so it went. He would move, we would move, then he would move again. This was great if you loved sports (new teams in Baltimore and Cincinnati!) but lousy for a marriage.

They finally got divorced on our eleventh move, but before then, the early years in Boston were wonderful. I always say I'm a child of the Red Sox and the Kennedys. By the time JFK—a millionaire's son from Harvard—emerged politically, we were deep into the mythology, and when the first Catholic was elected president, we watched the inauguration and cried with every word. I think my mother tried to join the Peace Corps at fifty years old.

We learned about the Kennedy–Fitzgerald dynasty early on, how Boston always had upper-crust mayors like John Phillips, Samuel Eliot, or two-time mayor Josiah Quincy before Irishmen like Collins and Honey Fitz took over. I was born in the Quincys' namesake city on September 11, 1953. Quincy was an early colonial settlement, founded in 1625, and was the birthplace of two U.S. presidents, John Adams and his son John Quincy Adams. All I cared about was that it was a ten-cent bus ride from Fenway. If my brother and I spent too much money at the game, we would walk home, a good ten miles. Once when we were walking, we stopped to sneak on to a miniature golf course. Another time, we brought my mother flowers that we'd pulled off some bushes near the bus stop.

The Red Sox were no good in my childhood, but it didn't matter. We were the team of Babe Ruth and Ted Williams. We thought we knew the truth on Ruth. Okay, he won us some World Series, but he was really a beer-guzzling, skirt-chasing, hot-dog-stuffing boor. Well, yes, his lifetime ERA was 2.28 and his winning percentage was .671. He hit with the power of a lumberjack and by the time he was nineteen, he was the best pitcher in baseball. He was still a Red Sox player then, and the stories we heard made us laugh. Like the time he punched an umpire and got a ten-game suspension, or when, on off days, he would drink all day and swim with his new bride. We even thought it was funny that he would shower and put on the same underwear. But when he went to the Yankees, we thought he was crude.

The Red Sox were nothing when he left, except for the sparkle of Ted Williams. I was born one month after Ted Williams came back to the Red Sox for the second time—after he'd done one tour of duty as a fighter pilot in World War II and another tour of duty in the Korean War. We'd hear about the '46 World Series, known for two things: that Ted Williams bunted and Enos Slaughter scored from first on his "Mad Dash Home." Of course, it was the winning run and the Red Sox lost to St. Louis. We whispered that yes, maybe Johnny Pesky held the ball too long, but when I met him years later I blithered like he was the best shortstop who ever lived. Williams was the greatest hitter and I will have that argument with anyone. He said he was a natural hitter because he took "a thousand swings a day." Yes, he was moody and could throw a fit. But his teammates said he was careful even there. When Williams would punch a locker, he would do it with his right hand. Of course, he was a lefty at the plate—ooh, that gorgeous swing from deep in his hips— although he did throw with his right hand. Curt Gowdy was the Red Sox play-by-play man my entire childhood, for fifteen years (1951–65), but he also did Super Bowls and Final Fours, Olympics, you name it. I was lucky to work for his son Curt Jr. at ABC, doing World Figure Skating, the World Series, and the Triple Crown. And Curt Jr. was kind enough to introduce me to his father on more than a few occasions. I even went to his house in Palm Beach once and pretended to like whiskey.

(Quick story, but fun. You know Saints quarterback Drew Brees? Do you know why he wears number 9? For Ted Williams! His father used to show him tapes of the Splendid Splinter at the plate, over and over, so Brees could see his hand-eye coordination and the way he shifted his weight. About seven years ago, I brought Drew a battered number 9 Red Sox cap, and he keeps it in his locker to this day.)

I and my brother Chris, who always listened to Red Sox games on the radio, went many times to Fenway Park to sit in the bleachers and eat Fenway Franks. The thirty-seven-foot-high Green Monster looked like the Great Wall of China to us. The Sox of the late fifties and early sixties were a bumbling group. The first black player, Pumpsie Green, would come in as a pinch runner for either Pete Runnels, who hit lefty but threw righty, or shortstop Don Buddin, who was once called "the most booed man in Boston." Willie Tasby spent exactly one season in center-field, and the manager's name was Pinky (Higgins). My favorite player was journeyman Ike Delock, a devoted right-hander who didn't even make it to the major leagues until he was twenty-two. With his cap pushed back on his head, he must have caught my eye one time, and

I've carried his number 14 (the pride of Highland Park, Michigan) ever since. I don't think he ever won more than fourteen games.

I never got to see Williams in person. My first visit to Fenway was in 1961. By then, "Teddy Ballgame" had retired. Everyone knows Curt Gowdy's call of Williams's famous last at-bat: "Everyone here in Fenway is quiet now after giving Williams a two-minute standing ovation . . . the count 1-1 . . . The drive to deep right—and it's gone— home run in Ted Williams's last at-bat!"

No, Williams didn't acknowledge the crowd after his home run; as John Updike so famously wrote in the *New Yorker*, "Gods don't answer letters." But what a résumé Williams left for us. He won the Triple Crown twice, was the last man to hit .400, and led the American League in batting six times. He went on to become a world-class fly fisherman with—who else?—Curt Gowdy.

It's odd that my most memorable game at Fenway—the game that subconsciously started me on this strange and wonderful path of wanting to be a sportswriter—was football, not baseball. In 1964, my father somehow got a couple of tickets to see the Boston Patriots play against the Oakland Raiders in Fenway Park. The football con-figuration was laid out left to right, covering the infield, with temporary bleachers set up in front of the Green Monster to seat five thousand fans.

It turned out to be one of the most memorable games in the AFL. A long-ball tie, 41–41, in the crisp October air. Babe Parilli and Gino Cappelletti flew up and down the field against Al Davis's black and silver Oakland Raiders.

I made my way down to the field (only a few feet from the stands) and I stood next to the biggest man I'd ever seen, the great lineman Jim Otto. When I became the first woman enshrined into the Pro Football Hall of Fame in 2006, Otto, now a longtime friend, whispered to me, "Pretty good for a girl who stood shivering on the sideline in Fenway." It was the moment I got hooked. I loved the game, I loved the time of year. I knew this was the place for me.

Today the Patriots are the equivalent of a Fortune 500 company behind the brilliant organization of Robert Kraft and his family, but when I was growing up, the Patriots were vagabonds, moving from Boston University to Boston College to Fenway Park to Harvard and finally, when I had the chance to cover them, to Foxborough. The stories of the early Boston Patriots were like something out of the Three Stooges. One player arrived driving a bus, followed by the state police because he'd plowed through the turnpike tolls. Running back Bob Gladieux, who'd been cut by the team, went to a game with his buddies anyway. Up in the stands, drinking beer, he heard the public address announcer say, "Would Bob Gladieux report to the locker room?" His friends were wondering where he'd gone when they heard, "Tackle on the kickoff made by number 24, Bob Gladieux." One year, like something out of a Mel Brooks movie, the Patriots were playing the Dallas Texans when someone in a trench coat swatted away the Texans' winning pass. Years later, Billy Sullivan, the glib and gutsy original owner of the Patriots, who always wore a trench coat, never denied it. Sullivan was never flush with cash. He once famously told the players not to turn down the bedsheets while taking a nap so the hotel wouldn't charge him an extra $10.

My family wasn't wealthy, either. Or anywhere close. We would buy a new pair of shoes for school at Kinney-on-the-Highway and some new clothes from Filene's, the oldest off-price retailer in the country. We'd drink Hood milk and honey-dipped donuts from Dunkin' Donuts, founded right there in Quincy. My mom got a job teaching at exclusive Derby Academy, the oldest coeducational school in the country, founded in 1784. Everyone was addressed as "Yes, Sir" and "No, Sir"; my classmates had names like Johnson (as in Howard) and Talbot (as in the store), and when they would go on vacations to places like St. Lucia, I'd be home reading the sports section. The art teacher at Derby, Doris Hauman, was the legendary illustrator of *The Little Engine That Could*.

Being in Boston year round did give me time to fall in love with the Celtics, who were unstoppable in the fifties and sixties. In the late fifties, I was crazy for six-foot-four Sam Jones, the Celtic shooting guard who was known as "Mr. Clutch." He was a small-town boy from North Carolina (Red Auerbach drafted him sight unseen), and he helped the Celtics win ten world titles. Everyone honored Bill Russell, as they should, but on Halloween, when other girls would dress up as Mary Poppins or Cinderella, I would go as Sam Jones, wearing high-cut Converse sneakers and the number 24 in Magic Marker on my T-shirt. Every year, Sam calls me and asks me not to do it anymore, but I don't care. I once did a radio show on Halloween wearing the authentic Celtic jersey that he'd finally given me.

With my idol Sam Jones, former guard of the great Boston Celtics. I wear his jersey every Halloween to this day. He begs me not to.

I had a depressing story many years later when Red Auerbach, who'd come to my wedding to Dick Stockton, refused to let me in the locker room just one year later, saying, "It's not for girls." It was yet another layer of scar tissue. I told him cigar smoke smelled terrible anyway, but I was crushed. I had to get quotes much later, when the players left the locker room, while hoping I didn't miss the deadline.

My family moved to Cincinnati when I was eleven years old. It was the true Midwest, where the people had easy temperaments (no rough edges), kind of like the Ohio River that flowed so easily. My brother and I went to Crosley Field, where the Reds played, a couple of times. Like Fenway, it was asymmetrical, fitting into the neighborhood, and it had a funny incline in left field. It actually rose up and was famously called "The Terrace." The NBA Royals had fantastic players like Oscar Robertson and Jerry Lucas, and my brother even cut Jack Twyman's lawn. I'd started reading *Sports Illustrated* and the *Sporting News*—articles about people I'd never get to see, like Y. A. Tittle, Cassius Clay, or John Wooden.

After the football experience in Fenway, and reading about people like Bill Bradley, I told my mother I wanted to be a sportswriter. This was 1965, and it was like saying I wanted to go to Mars, since the job didn't exist for women. Instead of my mom telling me it would be next to impossible, she said the greatest words I have ever heard: "Sometimes you have to cross when it says 'Don't Walk.'" It crystalized everything for me, changed my life in an instant. I was ready to lasso the moon.

CHAPTER 2

My parents' divorce came after I'd been shuttled to three different sixth grades. My mom packed up Chris and me and drove cross-country at about 38 mph, while terrified, to South Hadley, a bucolic eighteenth-century New England town. The home of Mount Holyoke College, one of the original Seven Sisters, South Hadley is a perfect place: a leafy town of rolling hills and maple trees centered among Smith College, Amherst College, and the University of Massachusetts, so everyone is either a farmer's kid or from the family of a professor. I didn't miss Ohio, although that's where my mom had given me the greatest opportunity of my life, telling me to cross when it says "don't walk." She'd even taken me to Stratford-upon-Avon that year to see Shakespeare's *Twelfth Night* and *A Midsummer Night's Dream*. She told me Shakespeare wrote for the masses, and even at eleven years old, I could handle the comedies. One day, she let me buy a miniskirt from the famous Carnaby Street in London, so my skinny knock-knees were the hit of Cincinnati. In South Hadley, though, with no money from my father, we lived in a lower-middle-class box house with two bedrooms (my mom called it "Treeless

Acres"), and she got a teaching job in nearby Granby, Massachusetts.

We were only ninety miles from Boston. No one drove there, but once she did the coolest thing. Remember when you'd take a class trip in high school to the museum or the aquarium? My mom rented a Peter Pan bus and took her class to Fenway Park! She called it a historical trip. We followed the Boston teams on the radio and sang along with pop music from WHYN out of Springfield ("Grazing in the Grass" or anything by the Beatles), and South Hadley was small enough that my brother and I captained every sport. One year, I was even voted the best athlete in the class, but I never talked about it to anyone. When you work with Phil Simms or Dan Marino or Bill Walton, you really don't want to talk about your MVP trophy from South Hadley High School.

The late sixties and early seventies were a tidal wave of social change. Golda Meir (raised in Milwaukee!) became the prime minister of Israel and Neil Armstrong walked on the moon. But they were also there when U.S. bombers secretly attacked Cambodia and Laos and more than 600,000 U.S. troops were fighting in Vietnam, many of them young people I knew. At South Hadley, we were let out of school for peace marches. I remember one afternoon we all met on the grassy green commons in the town center to sing "Give Peace a Chance" while holding white candles. We had no idea what Spiro Agnew was saying half the time, and we thought Nixon was from outer space. For the first time, most cars had air-conditioning. Not ours. My mother had a Dodge Dart, but it sat unused until Chris and I got our driver's licenses. Young women read Jane Austen and Gloria Steinem, and young men wanted books about hitchhiking and the universe. We put Sun-In in our hair and listened to weird lyrics from bands like the Flying Burrito Brothers. Concerts meant going to UMass to see Sly and the Family Stone. My mother taught Dostoevsky at night school at Mount Holyoke, and quoted the wits of the Algonquin Round Table and William Wordsworth ("The music in my heart I bore, / Long after it was heard no more"). I thought life was a blast, even if we didn't have any money.

Friday nights were for dances at the gym, where crummy high school bands played "Crimson and Clover" or "96 Tears." WHYN once mentioned my field hockey team (I was the captain) and you'd think I'd been recognized by the *Wall Street Journal*. We'd go to Mount Tom to ski in the winter and to eat cotton candy at the makeshift carnival in the summer. My friend Fizzy Plouffe ran the roller coaster for two months, and he'd let me go twenty times in a row without paying a dime. My high school boyfriend's family, the Newtons (whose earlier relations had invented Marshmallow Fluff!), had a house near Wildcat Mountain in New Hampshire, so we spent every New Year's freezing on the ski slopes, wearing only corduroy jeans and thin parkas, with maybe some hot chocolate between the long, cold runs.

I was neither great looking nor unattractive, but no one cared back then. High school wasn't really difficult for me; we had moved so many times that I knew how to fit in. I tried to write sports for the high school paper, but I got assignments like "What does the quarterback's girlfriend do while he's at practice?" Not for me—I wanted to cover UMass football games!

Being the daughter of an English teacher, I loved to read—Dickens, Wharton, Hemingway (much more than Fitzgerald)—and anything about the 1967 Red Sox "Impossible Dream" team. People in western Massachusetts followed them like a cult. The Sox had risen from ninth place to win the pennant under new manager Dick Williams. Carl Yastrzemski won the Triple Crown and "Gentleman" Jim Lonborg, the pitcher from Stanford, added twenty-two wins. The team was a cast of characters and Ken Coleman carried every game to us on radio. The season hit a sad note when Tony Conigliaro was hit in the left eye and cheekbone by Angels pitcher Jack Hamilton in early August. I remember I cried when I saw his picture in the paper, his face all swollen and bruised, his left eye shut tight. Conigliaro's agent, and eventually my good friend, Ed Kleven got Dionne Warwick and her pal Frank Sinatra to come to Boston and do a fund-raiser for Tony C! When he finally regained his sight, we were all relieved, and the season went back to being a celebration. The Red Sox won their first flag in twenty-one years and headed to the World Series for the first time since 1946. Of course, Curt Gowdy was the announcer, but this time for NBC. The Sox got all the way to Game 7—a dream matchup of Cy Young winner Lonborg against the legendary Bob Gibson. Lonborg, on only two days' rest, lost to the Cardinals Hall of Famer, 7–2. It would take Boston another three years to beat a St. Louis team—remember the glorious image of number 4, Bobby Orr, flying across the goal to beat the St. Louis

Blues in the Stanley Cup Final? All became right with the world.

The three of us, plus our extended Irish family, didn't watch much TV, except we'd all seen the aftermath of the Kennedy assassination back in 1963. That was when we lived in Boston, and it was a profound moment for everyone. The whole world became Bostonians twice in my lifetime: the JFK assassination and the Boston Marathon bombings. "Where were you when Kennedy was shot?" is still a question people ask to this day. I was in the fourth grade at Derby Academy and the headmaster let everyone out of school. My mother took us to a church in Hingham and I'll never forget the people sobbing over the altar, totally out of control. For days, everyone watched the news and the funeral. I don't remember any television before that. By high school, kids watched Johnny Carson if your parents let you stay up that late. But I loved *The Mary Tyler Moore Show* because she was a single girl with an important job, and five of the episodes were written by my friend Susan Silver. Other than that, I don't remember watching TV, except for some New York Giants games.

I didn't really know what I was doing in applying to colleges. My dad worked for the Stanford Research Institute, but I wasn't going to get into Stanford and I had no guidance about going to college or writing sports for a college paper. One guy from my high school, Marc Leonard, went to Boston College, so I called him. He liked it, so I applied. BC had everything I was looking for: great city, good school, big-time sports, and only four miles from the Green Monster. It wasn't like now, when parents take their kids on expensive road trips to look at schools. There was very little discussion in 1970. You picked a couple of schools and applied, $50 each. This was the hippie era, and people wanted to play the guitar ("House of the Rising Sun" or "Leaving on a Jet Plane") and just hang out. You couldn't tell who had money and who didn't. Everyone wore bell-bottom jeans and Indian print blouses and parted their long hair down the middle. We all wanted to look like Ali McGraw as Jenny Cavalleri in *Love Story*. The irony is that I married the *real* Oliver Barrett, her mythical boyfriend from Harvard. My husband, Bob Kanuth, is six foot four, gorgeous, and captained the '69 Crimson basketball team. He didn't even need a script.

I wore a crocheted hat, thinking I looked like Ali McGraw. I read whatever she read and quoted whatever she said. We also had many books around the house. I read anything: Ayn Rand's *We the Living* and *The Fountainhead* in the eighth grade, and I loved Herman Wouk's *Marjorie Morningstar*. I didn't understand, when I read Lillian Hellman's *The Children's Hour*, why two female teachers were always holding hands. My favorite books were *To Kill a Mockingbird* and *The Sun Also Rises*. I also loved *Basketball Is My Life* by Bob Cousy. I guess that was a little strange. My husband, Bob, gave me a first edition of *The Sun Also Rises* as a present one time. It sits on the bookshelf next to my signed basketball from Dave Cowens.

Boston College turned out to be a perfect place for me, with nice kids from all over the country, and I had easygoing roommates: Jeanne from Old Tappan, New

Jersey; Joan from Easton, Maryland; and Lori from Dixon, Illinois. We would read psychology books and debate politics, and sometimes I dragged them to Fenway. Jeanne put a poster on the wall of singer Grace Slick from Jefferson Airplane and I put up Tucker Frederickson, the standout player from Auburn who went on to be a running back with the New York Giants. Our dorm was off-campus freshman housing and looked like it hadn't been cleaned since the Depression. We didn't care. We bought eucalyptus branches, lit incense candles, and played David Bowie on someone's beat-up record player. We got along great.

In 1973, all my roommates gathered to watch Billie Jean King beat Bobby Riggs in three straight sets. I knew it was the seminal moment of the women's movement. It meant everything—social change, female strength, equal pay, gender politics, opportunity—a paradigm shift in perception. It was winner take all ($100,000) in Houston's Astrodome. Billie Jean entered the arena Cleopatra-style, carried high in a chair by men dressed as ancient slaves. Riggs gave King a giant lollipop and she gave him a pig.

Some said that Riggs threw the match, but the great player Jack Kramer wrote, "Billie Jean beat him fair and square. Men my age were so stunned when Riggs lost that they figure he must have tanked." But Billie Jean outhustled the hustler, continually giving him short balls that he was either too lazy or too out of shape to get to. In the beginning of the match, she ran Riggs from side to side, wearing him out. At the end—this, after he'd been on the cover of both *Sports Illustrated* and *Time* magazine— he told Billie that he'd underestimated her. The two of them were not all that different, really. Both had grown up in Southern California, he the son of a minister, she the daughter of a fireman. Both were great competitors and Wimbledon champions. More than 90 million people worldwide watched their match from the Astrodome. And some, like me, just knew it would change the culture.

The flip side of my pride in Billie Jean's victory was that I also worked at the BC college bar called Mary Ann's (still famous to this day), where the owner told me I had to wear orange hot pants and wait on young women who were trying to meet BC football players. I had a job bartending for a week, but when all the women would ask for complicated drinks, like Tequila Sunrises or Kahlua Sombreros, and I would just hand them a beer on tap, I got demoted to waitress. They left lousy tips, anyway.

I've grown to love Billie Jean and all that she stood for. In fact, she gave me some of the strongest words (outside my mother's) that I've ever heard in my life. They are words I try to live by. Billie Jean, brave enough to wear glasses as a professional athlete (unheard of except for Dom DiMaggio), was always in the Wimbledon Final—singles, doubles, mixed doubles—and she won twenty of them. I once asked her what the pressure was like of *always* being in the Wimbledon Final. Her answer changed the way I looked at life. It actually changed my way of thinking. She said, "Are you kidding? Pressure is a privilege!" From then on, I wanted the ball.

At BC I wrote sports for the college paper, called *The Heights*, and my editors were Mike Lupica and Lenny DeLuca—people I thought I'd never see again, but who

Winning the only Billie Jean King "Outstanding Journalist" award in Los Angeles in 2008

both went on to great success. They, of course, took all the good assignments, like football trips to Miami, and I was left with baseball double-headers (and believe me, Boston College baseball was no Texas).

In my junior year, I applied for a Carnegie Foundation Grant, given to twenty women in the country who wanted to go into jobs that were 95 percent male—which, really, were all *white-collar jobs*. This was 1973, not 1873, yet women were still mostly teachers, nurses, or secretaries. They were just starting to go to law school or medical school.

There were a series of interviews for the grant in Pittsburgh and New York. When they were complete, out of the twenty grant winners, one woman from Michigan got it for archeology, another woman from Radcliffe got it for anthropology—and I got it for sports-writing! Their heads must have been on a swivel, it was so unheard of.

The Carnegie Corporation would pay a stipend for eight weeks during the summer of 1974. I have never been to Carnegie Hall without saying a prayer of thanks for the great industrialist. (Andrew Carnegie is the greatest philanthropist in the history of this country except for Buffett and Gates, having donated more than a thousand libraries.) The grant entitled me to work anywhere in America, but I went to the paper with the best sports section in the country, the *Boston Globe,* and I thought I'd died and gone to heaven. The eagle had landed!

If I could save time in a bottle, I would save the summer of '74. The staff was world class: Bud Collins on tennis, Pete Gammons on baseball, Bob Ryan on basketball, Will McDonough on football, and columnists Ray Fitzgerald and Leigh Montville. The young reporters (now all Hall of Famers) were Kevin Dupont, Dan Shaughnessy, and me. We did a little bit of everything, and in the fall we covered high school sports.

I met Bud Collins in the fall of my junior year in college. I was a cheerleader at BC (I know it seems strange now, but this was before Title IX and was the only thing remotely athletic for women at the time). In the fourth quarter of a football game, Mike Lupica came down to the field and told me, "Get out of that cheerleader outfit, we're going to dinner with Bud Collins." I didn't know if he was kidding; I didn't even care. I ran up to my dorm

With legendary tennis writer Bud Collins at a 2007 dinner in Boston

room when the game ended and changed clothes. Mike and I took the T (Boston's public transit) to Newbury Street and went to this little French restaurant, two floors below street level, where they had things on the menu that I'd never heard of, like tournedos and chanterelles. There was Bud, and everything you've heard about him is true. He was the nicest man in the history of the business. He wasn't just the journalist who taught us all tennis. He was the socially conscious figure who traveled for a year with Muhammad Ali, defending him as a conscientious objector to the Vietnam War, and the man who went to South Africa with Arthur Ashe to combat apartheid. Bud cared about everything, from race relations to Vietnam to how your day went.

Bud died in March of 2016 at eighty-six, and he was a treasure to us all. He made tennis a major sport in this country, teaching us the backhand volley and making us laugh. He both educated and entertained—for fifty years at the *Globe*, and on NBC from 1972 to 2007. He made us get up for "Breakfast at Wimbledon." He said he went from being a scribbler to a babbler and I was lucky enough to start covering Wimbledon with him in 1976. Only a few American papers even traveled to Wimbledon in the late 1970s. It was a fantastic time for American tennis players: the rise of Chris Evert and Martina Navratilova; the stability of Billie Jean King; the emergence of John McEnroe, Bjorn Borg, and their elder, Jimmy Connors. The American correspondents had a small corner of the press room—we were called "the Colonials"—and we had to send our copy by Western Union. This wasn't the 1920s, but the 1970s. Bud famously tried, on one story, to write that girls in the stands loved Borg's flowing blond hair and went into fits of "Borgasms," but Western Union wouldn't send it. Bud didn't care. He had hundreds of other anecdotes and witticisms to fill the copy, anyway.

I loved college football, but I was meant for the pros. And in the early 1970s, the *Globe* made me the first woman to cover the NFL as a beat. It was both glorious and brutal. There are no other words. I cherished being near the greatest place on earth, an NFL kickoff, every Sunday at one o'clock, and I've tried to make humor out of all the slights that came with that privilege, slights that ranged from jealousy to contempt to no ladies' rooms to complete dismissal. I never sued anyone or went complaining to my editors, but it wasn't pretty. For one thing, the wives hated me. I was twenty-three years old, better than average looking (but by no stretch a beauty queen). It didn't help. The wives were sure I was after their men. I couldn't betray anyone—I needed the players' trust—so I never mentioned the clusters of groupies who greeted us in hotel lobbies in Kansas City, Oakland, and Buffalo.

I wanted to cover pro football for a variety of reasons. I loved the NFL. The game was exploding, overtaking baseball and horse racing, and it gave me the chance to show women that we could be something different than a nurse, a teacher, or a secretary. I also got to travel the country, places no one goes unless they are running for office or covering sports. When the *Globe* told me I'd be covering the Patriots, I almost fainted—I felt like the entire world of feminism was on my shoulders, but deep down I knew I would prove worthy of the task. Then I changed my outfit twenty-five times.

CHAPTER 3

I did a few features on the Patriots in 1975, months before I became the beat writer. That was a fantastic year to love sports or journalism. Watergate had come to its conclusion; Attorney General John Mitchell, along with Nixon's chief of staff H. R. Haldeman and lawyer John Ehrlichman had been found guilty of the cover-up and were going to prison. John Wooden coached his last game at UCLA by winning a national championship over Kentucky and, yes, a team called Golden State won the NBA title, beating the Washington Bullets in four straight games.

It was a time of basketball emergence. The Warriors, led by Hall of Famer Rick Barry, played in the Cow Palace, outside of San Francisco. The Bullets had two all-time greats, Elvin Hayes and Wes Unseld. Having interviewed both of them, I can tell you that Elvin could really sweat (not like Moses Malone, who would drip smelly droplets on me after a game) and Wes had the biggest rear end I've ever seen—way before the Kardashians. It was a fun time in America: the middle class was rocking along (to the sounds of KC and the Sunshine Band), and the general feeling was that people needed a hand up, not a hand out.

The year 1975 was the golden age of newspapers. Everyone had followed the Watergate hearings and wanted to be Woodward or Bernstein. The *Boston Globe* had already created the "Spotlight" team in the 1970s—the same group depicted in the Academy Award–winning film by that name in 2015. The legendary editor Tom Winship had created the investigative team decades before the current group uncovered the scandal in the Catholic Church. Spotlight even won a Pulitzer Prize in 1972 for exposing political favoritism in Somerville, Massachusetts. The *Globe*'s political cartoonist, Paul Szep, won the Pulitzer for editorial cartooning in 1974. Our sports department was filled with smoke and laughter, with a national following and the clatter of sportswriters on deadline. I pinched myself every day that I was a part of it.

It wasn't all glory. Our editors, Dave Smith and Vince Doria, along with the great assistant sports editor, Tom Mulvoy (who had a machine-gun mind and an appetite for any kind of knowledge), thought I was sort of a poor man's George Plimpton and would assign me humiliating first-person stories. Once I had to go hang gliding off some cliff in Plymouth. I nearly killed myself, but hang-gliding was cool and the *Globe* wanted a personal story on it. Another time, they sent me into the woods for three days for something called "orienteering." It was a sad form of competitive camping, thirty years before the internet or cell phones or help of any kind. As I recall, the competitors were supposed to sprint from point to point, using only a map and a compass. At night, we actually were given headlamps! I'm not making this up.

I didn't speak to Smith or Doria or Mulvoy for a month. As soon as I opened my mouth, though, they were back at it, making me go to a skateboarding stadium—a giant U-shaped arena where fearless kids on wooden boards with roller-skate wheels would push off the top of one end, fly down to the bottom, and let momentum carry them to the top of the other end. I told the photographer he better get it the first time, because I was only going to do it once. I have the scars of scraped knees to this day. I'm surprised Doria didn't think of making me try street luge.

I had a few more absurd assignments. One time I had to do a feature on a baseball player who had a tattoo of a bird and a worm on his inner elbow, and when he would flex his arm, the bird would eat the worm. No wonder I'd make Dan Shaughnessy go drinking with me at night. Dan was a great friend—someone who was safe, someone I could tell my deepest fears and my greatest triumphs to, and with whom I could share my childhood secrets. And we would laugh, God, we would laugh.

I lived with eight girls in two apartments in Brookline Village, a crummy space over the post office, so everyone woke up at 5 AM when the trucks would pull in beneath us to pick up the mail. My friend Jan and I would go up on the tar roof of the apartment building when it was 95 degrees and sing Elton John songs. We each had cheap guitars and thought we were Joan Baez. Across from us was an Irish bar, and we'd go sing "Four Green Fields" like we'd come to America in the potato famine. Jan was Scottish, and I was Dutch, but we didn't care.

While everyone was living and dying with the Red Sox, the *Globe* sent me to Shea Stadium, where the Giants, Yankees, Mets, and Jets were all playing in one year in one stadium. It was crazy—people don't remember, but under new Yankee owner George Steinbrenner, it was announced that Yankee Stadium would undergo two years of renovation and the team would have to play at Shea. Picture all four teams playing in one facility, juggling schedules and dates and billboards. Shea had a Kentucky bluegrass outfield and a dirt infield. No one on the grounds crew, led by Pete Flynn, had a day off for more than a year. It was twelve months of scheduling nightmares, field issues, locker room sharing (the Yankees thrown in with the Jets), and media competition. Bill Virdon was the manager of the Yankees, and the players complained that the dimensions were so much bigger at Shea than at Yankee Stadium that they couldn't hit home runs. No one came to the games, even though the Yankees had Catfish Hunter and Bobby Bonds. The planes overhead, waiting to land at La Guardia Airport, bothered the pitchers and, of course, there was no room on the scoreboard for an American League DH. I thought it was funny, and I was glad to get back to Fenway.

The year 1975 also led to one of my favorite arguments: What do you think the greatest sporting event of your lifetime was? The Thrilla in Manila, Secretariat, the Miracle on Ice? My husband, who grew up in Columbus, Ohio, would say the it was the last-second Buckeye win over Michigan in 2016. To me, without question, it was Game 6 of the 1975 World Series—a game that began on Tuesday, October 21, but actually ended, as Sinatra would say, "In the Wee Small Hours of the Morning" of Wednesday, October 22.

Fans had started paying real attention to the Red Sox that September. They were obviously headed for the playoffs; I did stories on rookies Fred Lynn and Jim Rice, the golden twins who were so integral to the Sox title chase. Rice missed the playoffs with a broken hand, but he helped get them there. Lynn, of course, was the Rookie of the Year and the MVP in the same season, and he was both polite and kind. Luis Tiant had been rescued from the scrap heap years before, yet he led the Sox to two wins over the Reds in the World Series. Before the games, he would wander the stands and pose for pictures. There was even an El Tiante Cubano Sandwich—twenty-five years before stadiums started having specialty foods—and people wore fake Fu Manchu mustaches in his honor.

The sixth game of the 1975 World Series followed a three-day rain delay. On Tuesday, October 21, 1975, the skies finally cleared. It was game time. Cincinnati manager Sparky Anderson popped a piece of gum in his mouth at 6 AM, and All-Star catcher Johnny Bench felt lousy, but he knew it was the day. Luis Tiant shook off his own cold; it was late October and, for *everyone*, it was cold. Fred Lynn had watched *Monday Night Football* the night before (he could have played football at USC) and he didn't get much sleep. It had been five days since both teams played in Cincinnati. The *Globe* had everyone on duty—fifteen story lines—would the Carmine Hose finally win at home against the Big Red Machine?

I was a twenty-one-year-old graduate of Boston College. Sports, especially baseball, had been a man's game, and I was glad to be part of the periphery. I was not included in the vast array of assignments, but Peter Gammons, whom I will love until the day I die, said that he and Tony Kubek of NBC had an extra credential—would I like to go to the game? Cue the archangels. I was insane with joy, and I went to the press box on Tuesday night three hours early and sat there like a statue.

The tarp over the infield had been put on and pulled off at least five times and Joe Mooney, the famous groundskeeper, finally said the field was ready to go. Chet Simmons, head of NBC, knew that the last three World Series had been won by Charles Finley's colorful but small-market Oakland Athletics, and that this game had the chance to be really big time. A gibbous moon (I looked it up—it means the moon and the sun are on opposite sides of Earth) hung over Fenway.

Before the game, I had been introduced to announcer Dick Stockton, who was calling the game for NBC. He barely acknowledged me, but said maybe some night we could have dinner. I thought he was smart and funny—who else would be asked to do the World Series? But both of us were otherwise occupied.

Cincinnati had a 3–2 lead in the Series. Bernie Carbo's pinch-hit three-run homer tied the game in the eighth inning, 6–6, and things really got tense. Dwight Evans robbed Joe Morgan of the go-ahead run in the eleventh inning with a spectacular catch in right field and it was still tied, deep into a crisp October night.

When Carlton Fisk came up to face Pat Darcy in the bottom of the twelfth, no one knew his home run and body language would become the stuff of lore. Fisk had been born across the Massachusetts state line in Bellows Falls, Vermont, and was raised in Charlestown, New Hampshire. He'd played baseball at Charlestown High and had been called "Pudge" from the time he was eight years old. With his massive shoulders and square jaw, he told people that he would never give up and never give in.

Dick Stockton called Fisk's titanic blast down the left field foul pole, saying, "If it stays fair, home run!" Bells rang out all over New England, especially in Charlestown. The organist at Fenway, John Kiley, played Handel's *Hallelujah* chorus. It was 1:15 AM, and a son of New England had hit one of the most famous home runs in baseball history. Harry Coyle's famous use of the left field scoreboard camera caught Fisk willing the ball to stay fair. Because of that shot, baseball changed. Networks refigured where they would put their cameras, and reaction shots became standard stuff. Not only was Game 6 one of the best games ever played—it was certainly, to that point, the best baseball broadcast.

Dick Stockton and I did go out for that dinner a week later, and he related the story of how, as a thirty-two-year-old broadcaster, he got a telegram saying that NBC would like him to do the World Series. It was from legendary producer Chet Simmons, who also wished Dick luck. After many days of rain, Bowie Kuhn decided that going up against *Monday Night Football* and *All in the Family* wasn't a good trade for twenty-four more hours, so that is why Game 6 was finally played on Tuesday night. Dick had done Game 1, then Simmons had a rotation among Curt Gowdy and Joe Garagiola. It just happened that Dick had Game 6. We used to joke that meeting me (we were

At home in front of a painting given to me by my husband in 2011. Photo by Joe Fistick ©2016 SportsBusiness Journal. All rights reserved. Reprinted with permission.

married for twenty-six years) wasn't even the greatest thing that happened to Dick that *night*! A week after the series, Dick took me to the famous Cafe Budapest. Someone at the *Globe* had put a note in my typewriter: "Before you think you like Dick Stockton, you should know that he's been to the Cafe Budapest three times in the last week with three different girls." When I confronted Dick with this, he said, sheepishly, "I like the chicken paprikash."

CHAPTER 4

I've been blessed in my life to have had two great husbands. I was a young *Boston Globe* reporter when I met Dick Stockton at the sixth game of the '75 World Series, and I was fifty-six years old when I went to say hello to Rick Pitino at the Kentucky Derby and he introduced me to my lifetime love, Bob Kanuth. Dick and I were married for almost twenty-six years, and now Bob and I are going on eight. And while I've had plenty of regrets, those men aren't two of them.

Dick's had a forty-five-year broadcasting career characterized by class and the comprehension of his role—not too much, not too little. He grew up listening to broadcasters like Russ Hodges and Ernie Harwell. I think the greatest day of his life was October 3, 1951—known in baseball as "the Shot Heard 'Round the World." Dick was nine years old when New York Giants third baseman Bobby Thomson hit the game-winning home run off Dodger Ralph Branca at the Polo Grounds in the first-ever nationally televised game.

Dick heard it on the radio—Russ Hodges's famous call, "The Giants win the pennant, the Giants win the pennant!"—and every year on October 3, we used to make a pilgrimage to where the Polo Grounds used to be so I

With Hall of Fame Coach Rick Pitino, who won NCAA titles with both Kentucky and Louisville, at the 2010 Kentucky Derby

could hear the whole story . . . again. Thomson's dramatic three-run homer in the ninth inning (with Willie Mays on deck) was also known as "The Miracle of Coogan's Bluff," coined by legendary sportswriter Red Smith. Of course, being born in Boston, I always thought the "Shot Heard 'Round the World" was from Ralph Waldo Emerson's poem about the first battle of the Revolutionary War between Lexington and Concord, but once I threw in with Dick, the phrase took on a new meaning.

To be honest, I think our marriage was solid because we only saw each other three days a week. Can you imagine? But it was true; both of us loved our careers, which meant crisscrossing the country for the *Globe* for

With former husband Dick Stockton in front of the Blue Mosque in Istanbul in 1992

Traveling with my former husband Dick Stockton on a ferry to Morocco in 1998

sporting events and appearances. Dick said we didn't
fight because by the time we saw each other, we'd forgotten what the argument was about anyway.

Sometimes we worked together, like the legendary
Celtics–Lakers Finals, or on a football or baseball game—
even the Olympics. I remember one time during the ALCS
in the early nineties, Dick, Jim Kaat, and I were doing a
Twins playoff game in Minnesota and Dick said, "Let's
go to Lesley Visser for a report." Kaat asked, "Why don't
you just say 'my wife'?" Dick and I lived in Manhattan
for most of our years together, although we also had a
home in Florida. I never cooked, ever—not as a child,
not in college, not in my career. My current husband,
Bob, is a fantastic cook, so I'm still on cleanup duty in
my sixties. But I remember *Vogue* magazine coming to
our New York apartment to do a story on how I used the
stove as an extra rack for my sweaters. If people asked
Dick if I cooked, he'd say, "Sure, last night we had baked
cashmere."

Our apartment on Sutton Place was huge, taking up
an entire floor, with five and a half bathrooms, plenty
of bedrooms, a home gym, and two living rooms, which
meant we had lots of company and ordered lots of takeout.
Dick was born in Philadelphia, moved early to New York,
and went to Syracuse University, home of great broadcasters like Marty Glickman, Marv Albert, Bob Costas, and
Mike Tirico. When I first heard of Dick, he had just become
the Red Sox television announcer, but I didn't meet him
until that magical game in '75 when he called Fisk's home
run for NBC. After our one date at the Cafe Budapest, I'd
see him across the court at different events, but we never

Before having a drink with Dick Stockton and Jack Nicholson in Paris, where Nicholson was filming *Something's Gotta Give*

really talked again until a 1982 Laker game, when we were both staying in the same hotel in Los Angeles. A couple of months later, we were in New York and he asked me to marry him. I think we were both so flustered that we went into some bar on Second Avenue and knocked back shots of tequila. It was an easy marriage—we could talk sports or politics, and Dick could play Gershwin or show tunes on the piano. Both of us loved the theater and great Italian restaurants, and traveling was much simpler back then. By 2010, a wonderful marriage had turned into a wonderful friendship—I deeply respected that Dick had become one of the most recognizable voices in sports, calling play-by-play at the highest level. But I think we started to look at each other as excellent professionals, not lifelong partners.

Then, la-dee-da, life intervened for us—now both happily remarried. When I was only twenty-one, the *Boston Globe* assigned me to be the beat writer for Rick Pitino, who was the twenty-two-year-old kid coach of the Boston University Terriers. It was a blast. Rick tried all kinds of defenses because no one was watching, and I tried all kinds of coverage because no one was reading. I became great friends with Rick and his wife Joanne, and I continued both to follow and cover his career, including

With my husband Bob Kanuth at the 2012 Real Deal Awards in New York. Photo by Tim Kuratek/CBS ©2012 CBS Broadcasting Inc. All rights reserved.

Crossing Harvard Yard with husband Bob Kanuth

all seven of his Final Fours at Providence, Kentucky, and Louisville.

Fast-forward to the 2010 Kentucky Derby. I went to Rick's box—on the finish line of Millionaire's Row, befitting the championship coach—to say hello to his family and friends. He had his usual suspects there: buddy Steve Alaimo, a handful of Maras (the owners of the New York Giants), some former players, his money man Tom Healy, and his jeweler Joe Iracane. He even had the singer Meat Loaf! At one point, Rick wandered over and said, "Lesley, you have to meet a friend of mine, Bob Kanuth; he was the captain of Harvard Basketball in 1969."

Well, I said to myself, *I don't think so*, since I've covered thirty NCAA Tournaments and his name had never come up. I stuck my hand out forcefully and announced, "I doubt you were the captain of Harvard Basketball since I've never heard of you," and Bob, all elegant six-foot-four of him, said quietly, "You must have missed four years."

I can hear you laughing, I can see your pity. Yes, it was not pretty. And every time people ask how we met, Bob just looks at me. I blame Pitino.

CHAPTER 5

B ecause there were no provisions for equality when I started (known everywhere as, "Did you go in the locker room?"), I had to wait outside in the parking lots for the athletes or coaches instead of going with the other journalists. And from Chicago to Green Bay to Buffalo, it was plenty cold standing in those parking lots.

With the late, great *Boston Globe* football writer Will McDonough

Reporting outside the Chicago Bears' Soldier Field

I remember one day in December 1977, when I thought my Boston was the coldest place on earth. It was after the Patriots–Dolphins game, and with no other women and no chance to be inside the locker room with the other writers, I was outside in 10-degree weather, wind chill –5. While waiting, I remember thinking, "If I go find a bathroom, I might miss Sam Cunningham going to his car," or "If I'm over near the Dolphins bus trying to get Bob Griese, Steve Grogan might slip by and get in his Jeep, and I'll never hear from the winning quarterback." It was a trap on many levels, but it was part of what came with the privilege of covering the New England Patriots as a beat writer for the best sports section in America when newspapers were in their golden era.

Interviewing the great football legend Don Shula

I'm not exaggerating about the cold or the literary climate. In 2009, *Sports Illustrated* named the *Boston Globe* sports section from the mid-seventies to the mid-eighties (exactly when I was there) the "greatest collection of reporting talent ever assembled, unrivaled in its time and surely never to be duplicated today." Will McDonough, our Hall of Fame NFL writer, told legendary editor Dave Smith, "Get us money, get us space, and get out of the way." To this day, I have columnist Ray Fitzgerald's first draft of Game 6 of the '75 World Series. I was in the press box, not moving because I so desperately appreciated the ticket, but when Bernie Carbo came to bat as a pinch hitter in the bottom of the eighth with two men out and two men on, and the Sox trailing Cincinnati 6–3 and 3–2 in games, and Carbo blasted a three-run homer, Fitzgerald ripped the paper from his typewriter and let it fall to the floor. Like some kind of groupie, I groped around and picked it up. His lede, written after the seventh inning, said simply, "You could feel it slipping away." For me, it was like finding a first edition of *To Kill a Mockingbird*.

Being in the Schaefer Stadium parking lot waiting for a Patriot was no different than being at Rich Stadium in Buffalo or Lambeau Field in Green Bay. I was caught in what John Madden used to say was a "two-way go." I didn't want to complain to the *Globe*, because they'd given me the cherished assignment of being the first female NFL beat writer in the country, and I didn't want to protest to the Patriots lest they tell the paper, "See, we told you a woman couldn't do this job." So there I'd stand, hopping from one cold foot to the other and not wearing gloves because they were too bulky to wear while writing down what the players said. I suppose I could have tried some *Yentl* thing, dressing up as a boy, but I don't think I could have cut it. And I didn't know any Yiddish.

Standing in parking lots was kind of an existential loneliness. I was divided from my colleagues. That separation made me feel alone and apart, and I had no remedy. It was an unsupported existence. But covering these games, my lifelong dream, was like oxygen to my brain. Some of the solitary confinement was even good for me. I had to think about which questions I would ask which players, not just stick a microphone in a player's face behind a pack of journalists who never even make eye contact. I had to do it all myself and trust that I'd be getting the readers of the *Boston Globe* the right information. It taught me to have real appreciation for the athletes and the job, and it crystalized my natural curiosity.

Of course there were times when athletes wanted to take it further—dinner, drinks, or a romp in the hotel room. And I had one famous exchange with Bert Jones, the quarterback of the Baltimore Colts. By any standard, Jones was gorgeous. He'd been the second pick of the 1973 NFL draft, a legend from LSU. After the Patriots–Colts game in 1976, he asked if I wanted a round-trip ticket to Baltimore, and I went into my Gloria Steinem routine: "Absolutely not! This is my job, I do *not* dance with quarterbacks!"

Bert just laughed, brushed my shoulder, and said, "Hey, you're not that great anyway." What? I was mortified, and I think Miss Alabama was over by the bus, looking to meet him. There were no quick fixes to the postgame formula because locker rooms weren't open for another six years—and that had its own challenges, which I'll get to later.

There wasn't a category of therapy to deal with being the first to do something (I didn't think I could call African American tennis pro and Wimbledon trailblazer Althea Gibson), and the guys at the *Globe* just wanted to play pickup basketball or argue about Williams and DiMaggio. Dave Smith, and later Vince Doria, put together a 1927 Yankees lineup—Peter Gammons on baseball and Bob Ryan on basketball—and both started on the very same day, one a graduate of North Carolina, the other from Boston College. Tennis god Bud Collins had fought for social justice with Ali and Arthur Ashe. Dan Shaughnessy, Kevin Dupont, and I covered high school football in 1975. All-around writer John Powers won a Pulitzer Prize. McDonough once even punched Patriot cornerback Ray Clayborn in the locker room because Clayborn pushed him and complained that the reporter pack had gotten too close. Another *Globe* sportswriter, Leigh Montville, said he was terrified a brawl would break out, so he went looking for the field-goal kicker.

Being alone outside meant I missed all that, but the long-term results were that I went to thirty-five Super Bowls, thirty-five Final Fours, fifteen Wimbledons, and ten Olympics, plus the NBA Finals, the World Series, and the Triple Crown. I used the same humor approach—Rick Pitino once called it my "wit and charm offensive"—in every sport, and it provided a balm for sports' slings and arrows. After writing and filing the report, or going out with the other writers, I'd go back to the hotel room

Reporting from the 2011 Final Four in Houston. ©2011 CBS
Broadcasting Inc. All rights reserved.

and let both the happiness and the hollowness wash over me. Even though I was often isolated, it was the career I wanted. And it more than returned the favor.

But The Locker Room—those three little words—dominated my life in sports for fifteen years. For the first seven or eight years, there were no provisions for women, so I stood in those parking lots after games, waiting for the athletes. It wasn't even a discussion. Women and children had struggled as cheap labor—no property rights, no right to vote—for hundreds of years. We finally won the right to vote in 1920, but entering a locker room must have seemed a thousand years away! I remember reading Betty Friedan's *The Feminine Mystique*, which chronicled the emotional and intellectual oppression experienced by people like my mother, a teacher who could have been a university president. I think it galvanized me.

Many people think I'm a product of Title IX, but I actually owe much of my career to the women's movement, specifically the Equal Rights Amendment. I remember being about a junior in high school when, with a group of my girlfriends, I took a bus to Washington to march for equal rights. I was so excited that Gloria Steinem was there, although we never got near her. She later asked me to write one or two articles for *Ms.* magazine and I thought I'd won the Pulitzer Prize. The National Organization for Women argued that women had the right to apply for any job for which they were qualified, and they took the argument all the way to the Supreme Court.

Things were happening in the late seventies, all to the good. Women were being hired as sportswriters, not for their looks, but for their ability to get the story, get it on deadline, and get it right. I didn't see many of these women near the beginning, but they were coming, and when Title IX was passed in 1972 and kicked in for generations of women after that, the dam had been broken and there was no going back.

The first two locker rooms I went in, at about the same time, were those of the Boston Lobsters, who played team tennis at Boston University's Walter Brown Arena, and Holy Cross after a basketball game. Two extremely enlightened men made it possible: first Robert Kraft, who now owns the gold-standard New England Patriots (and about whom I'll write more in Chapter 7), and George Blaney, the coach at Holy Cross. Not many people went to see the Lobsters, but it was a great training ground, and people like Martina Navratilova were on the team. I was the beat writer for the *Globe*, and I also did quite a few Holy Cross games, with my typewriter in one hand and a fax machine in the other. I would memorize my questions before I went into the locker room so no one could accuse me of looking around, and if I forgot a question, so be it. I just pivoted and left.

By the way, it wasn't some Chippendale's in there; it was hot and sweaty and everyone, both players and journalists, wanted to get the work done and get out of there. In 2013, ESPN devoted a whole documentary, "Let Them Wear Towels," to the first women who broke down the locker room barriers. It was one of the major battles in feminist history, but it's completely taken for granted. I often look at so-called women's magazines and they rarely, if ever, do stories about women who cover sports.

And if they do a story about Venus or Serena Williams, it's almost always about their clothing line.

"Let Them Wear Towels" got a lot of attention in 2013, just as the subject did in the 1970s and 1980s. Opponents of women entering the locker room claimed it would violate the players' privacy—we were seen as voyeurs. Then we would argue that the locker room is the place of business after a game—that's where the quotes are, that's where the game is analyzed by players and coaches. It was obvious that 75,000 fans couldn't be in there to hear the players' reactions, so our press passes gave us that responsibility. It's where the stories are.

Much of it in the beginning was ugly, but all of us know that this wasn't ISIS or child slavery—we were covering sports. Still, it was a frontier. Melissa Ludtke, covering baseball for *Sports Illustrated*, said she felt "like a stranger in a strange land"—quoting the title of a popular book at the time. One day, she talked her way into manager Billy Martin's office and sat there until she was thrown out. She was told that she was not to go anywhere near the clubhouse because Commissioner Bowie Kuhn had decided that the players' wives would be embarrassed or ridiculed. In 1977, Time, Inc., the parent company of *Sports Illustrated*, sued the Yankees under the Fourteenth Amendment (the right to do your job with equal protection under the law) on Melissa's behalf to enter the locker room. Time won. The *Boston Globe* sent me the day the Yankee clubhouse opened, and Melissa and I have been good friends to this day.

You must remember this was before Google, Twitter, Facebook, or cell phones. We were all operating on just the engines of our brains. The first generation of women sportswriters included Ludtke at *SI*, Betty Cuniberti in San Bernardino, Michelle Himmelberg in Tampa, Robin Herman at the *New York Times*, and myself at the *Globe*. We all had embarrassing stories. I remember once, when quarterback Jim McMahon was with the Philadelphia Eagles, he told me to come to his locker, that he had a Christmas present for me. I was shocked and delighted, thinking it would be some cookies or maybe candy canes. All the players gathered around and McMahon fished through the bottom of his locker until he found the holiday box. He handed it to me, smiling, and told me to open it.

It was a black negligee.

I was horrified, and I know every woman in this business also has had moments of great discouragement. The next generation of women were equally talented: Christine Brennan, Ann Liguori, Sally Jenkins, Jackie MacMullan, Johnette Howard, Cindy Shmerler, Susan Fornoff, Kristin Huckshorn, and Melissa Isaacson. Brennan famously used to say that going in the locker room meant "you had to be a little deaf." She'd remember taunts like "Take a bite of this"—"things they would be arrested for on the street corner." Fornoff covered the Oakland A's for the *Sacramento Bee* in 1985, and Dave Kingman would constantly belittle her, often ignoring her questions. The next year, Kingman famously left Fornoff a rat in a box with the tag, "My name is Sue."

In 1990, many years after we'd been going in and out of locker rooms, Lisa Olson, the talented writer for the *Boston Herald*, was subjected to boorish behavior by some of the New England Patriots. Lisa called it "mind rape," and the Patriots were fined a mere $25,000. The players were fined $12,000. This was before Robert Kraft owned the team—he'd never have put up with it. Even the legal system didn't cleanse Lisa; she fled to Australia. But what does that say? One player was later signed by the New York Giants, and Olson moved halfway around the world. Is that what Susan B. Anthony marched for? I used to say to people, you wonder why we drink! By 1990, I had gone to CBS and *The NFL Today*, and thanks to executives there like producer Ted Shaker, sexism and discrimination were not tolerated.

There were times, though, that the challenges remained. In the early 1990s, Jenny Kellner of the *New*

With Deion Sanders of CBS Sports. ©2002 CBS Worldwide Inc. All rights reserved.

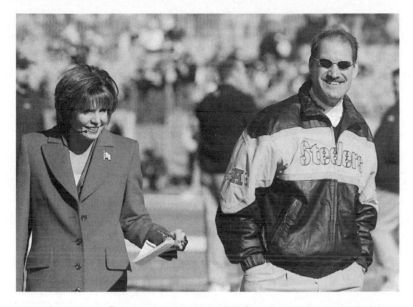

With Pittsburgh Steelers head coach Bill Cowher before the 2002 AFC Championship Game in Pittsburgh. Photo by Rusty Kennedy/CBS

York Daily News faced down New York Jet Mark Gastineau with an oft-repeated remark, one I'd never have the guts to say. When Gastineau, the star defensive end, showed his privates to Kellner and asked, "Do you know what this is?" she famously replied, "It looks like a penis, only smaller." Now that was a confident demeanor, no matter how she felt inside. I remember doing a story on the Jets a few years before that, and when I walked into the locker room, tight end Mickey Shuler yelled out about a "broad being in here looking around." CBS, Shaker, and the Jets did not let it stand. Shuler wrote me a heartfelt apology, but I always tell young women that no one teaches you a class in humiliation. You study, you pay attention, you ask the right questions (with the notepad not far from your nose, so no one suspects anything), but that doesn't mean you'll always be accepted. There will be times when you do everything right and someone will still make you feel like a creep, like something dirty or unworthy. I don't think he was thinking about us, but in 1967 when Cat Stevens sang the song, "The First Cut is the Deepest," he had it right.

In the end, any experience changes you, and experiences are good for that. The trick is to own that moment. Almost everyone has a different interpretation of this. The legendary coach Red Auerbach used to say, "If you're going to keep score, you might as well win." The Persian poet Rumi said life has three staples, love, knowledge, and the law, and he found love to be the most important. I always thought humor helped me get along—it lightened the load, it defused the tension, it (mostly) diverted the hurt. But everyone has to find a path.

CHAPTER 6

We all remember that Donald Trump revived "locker room" talk in his presidential campaign. In 2016, female Harvard soccer players who were the subject of a sexually explicit "scouting report" by the men's team wrote an op-ed for the *Harvard Crimson* saying, essentially, "the world is a locker room." It brought down the male team. The men of Harvard (of all places!) apologized to the women for "rating their appearance" and assigning them "sex positions." For about forty-five minutes, all was right with the world.

But has it changed? The basic first step for female sportswriters and broadcasters was to get hired, then we had our own zigzag paths. My Terry Bradshaw story is near legendary in the annals of women covering sports. In the late 1970s, without provisions for equal access after a game, I was in my usual spot—in the parking lot—this time outside freezing Three Rivers Stadium in Pittsburgh. Bradshaw, the quarterback, finally emerged and saw me. He took my notebook, signed an autograph, and hustled away. I was left slack-jawed, stammering, "But—but, I'm a reporter!" Terry, now one of my good friends for decades, said that his autograph was worth more than "any crap

I was going to write in the *Boston Globe*." I think he said it with a smile.

A little history. The first modern Olympics were for men only, but in 1900 women were allowed to participate. Over the years, the Games were flexible—tug-of-war was weeded out and the women's marathon was added in Los Angeles in 1984. Professional athletes are now able to compete. I became the first woman to go down the Olympic bobsleigh (bobsled) in 1992 in Albertville, France, when the U.S. Team invited me. I had to get written permission from the president of the Games, Jean-Claude Killy, and the head of the United States Olympic Committee, Harvey Schiller. The thinking had been that women's trapezius muscles (top of the shoulder) weren't strong enough for our neck and head to withstand the g-forces going down the run and that our necks would snap back. I agreed to go down in the four-man bobsled (I was in the third position—remember Herschel Walker was on the team?) and all I kept thinking was that line from Bob Seger's "Against the Wind"—"Wish I didn't know now what I didn't know then." It was terrifying, rattling around in that skinny tin can. l was bruised for two weeks and I looked like bad fruit, but I lived to tell the tale.

As the Olympics has successfully adapted and endured, so have women who cover sports. It's not been easy, nor has it been a straight path. But women have had a passion and a skill, proving themselves over the years, and a handful of men in the 1970s took a chance on us. We had early rallying cries of equal opportunity and equal pay, but the truth is, if we got the job, most of us didn't care about the money. The job had its own unique challenges— with no role models—so getting a byline in the paper

Covering Prince Albert at the 1992 Olympic bobsled venue La Plagne in Albertville, France. He was a member of Monaco's team.

First woman down the bobsled run during the 1992 U.S. Olympic team's practice run in Albertville, France

Speaking at a 2009 event for young women in New York

was triumph enough. Women are still only 13 percent of sports departments, both newspaper and broadcast, and very few women are in positions of executive power. In forty years, I have never been hired by a woman, and only in 2016 at CBS was I able to pitch my story ideas to a fantastic female producer, Emilie Deutsch, a woman I'd worked with at ABC some twenty-five years before.

The early years were full of nerves and disappointments, yet many nights were filled with laughter and celebration. The first handful of women were so close that we were on each other's holiday lists. We used to say, "We will have made it when we all don't know each other!" Well, that time has come. The fight for access and status has resulted in women not even giving a second thought as to how they'll get in the press box, or where they'll go to the bathroom. Sometimes there is even a line! Women today, for the most part, can focus on the job, not wondering if there will be some ugly incident or access denial. After Robin Herman, covering professional hockey for the *New York Times*, and Marcel St. Cyr, a Montreal-based radio reporter, broke the locker room barrier in 1975, Herman received a handful of letters calling her a "prostitute." That's not the scene today, although many people, Herman among them, are dismayed that women are on the sideline and not in the booth.

I love her impatience. As the person who invented the sideline role for women (I replaced three men—Irv Cross at CBS, Jack Whitaker on the Kentucky Derby, and Lynn Swann on *Monday Night Football*), I appreciate the job. Think of it. There are only three people *total* on a broadcast and the person on the sideline is one of them. I admit, in some ways, the job *has* diminished; some even consider it a dumping ground for women. It used to be a real reporter's job, the gathering of information unavailable to the men in the booth. In many instances now, the job has been reduced to sticking a microphone in or near the player's face for his or her response.

The optimist in me knows how difficult that job is. You have no idea, at the end of a game, what a scrum it is out there in the middle of the field, how complicated it is to get the player you want, keep your wits about you, and be mindful of holding the player in place through a commercial break. Then the job starts. I was the first woman to provide color in an NFL booth (2001, the Dolphins) and on *Monday Night Radio* (Westwood One,

Reporting from the field at Super Bowl XLVII in New Orleans

2000), but although these opportunities, like being the first woman on the sideline, were huge breakthroughs, neither appealed to me. I'm a reporter at heart, and that's the path I've followed, but I believe a lot of social progress has been made. A young girl can now say I want to cover football or baseball, I want to be in print or on TV. I want to be a director, like Suzanne Smith at CBS, who handles a truck for NFL games, or a producer like Emilie Deutsch.

The athletes themselves have made a change. Decades ago, they would scream about a woman being in their space. Now, for the most part, they accept that reporters will be there to get the story. There are eighty-two games in the NBA's regular season and almost twice that many in Major League Baseball, and athletes only care if the same questions are being asked over and over again, as waves of journalists advance to their locker. It doesn't bother them, it bores them. Even when the NFL locker rooms became open to women in the early-to-mid 1980s, more players were respectful than those who tried to make a scene. Many franchises now have their own media teams and their own studios, and a good number of those reporters are women. I call that progress.

Progress, yes, but so much more to do. Amid the big sports headlines in 2016 about the Golden State Warriors and the Oakland Raiders, there was a small note in the *New York Times* that said, "Princeton cancels the remainder of the season in swimming and diving" . . . because

With CBS director Suzanne Smith at dinner in 2010. She is the only woman currently directing NFL games.

team members had posted "vulgar and offensive" material about women on their electronic mailing list. Sound familiar? In the same year that Simone Biles took gymnastics to a nearly inhuman level, when Katie Ledecky pushed the pace in the pool faster than the cars at Indy, schools from Harvard to Amherst—oh, did I mention that Amherst College suspended its men's cross-country team after reports that the athletes made racist and misogynistic comments in team-wide emails? Where was I? It was a year that a woman was nominated for president, a year that inspired more women to seek higher office, yet the tweets of Donald Trump took center stage.

There was a time before Facebook, which was founded in 2004, and Twitter and Instagram (2006 and 2010, respectively), when opinion makers had to attach their names to anything they wrote. Women make up 51 percent of the U.S. population and account for 47 percent of the labor force, yet many women don't even root for each other. In many ways, we're still swimming upstream. Katy Perry has more than 97 million Twitter followers, yet athletes from small, academically accomplished schools are still rating women on their looks. There is no way to counter that Lesley Stahl has to look great while doing a great job (in places like Syria, no less!), while Morley Safer and Andy Rooney never had to look anywhere near as stylish. Maybe we should all listen to the late, great Carrie Fisher, who said, "Please stop debating about whether or not I aged well . . . it hurts all three of my feelings." Okay, maybe, as Carrie continued, "my body hasn't aged as well as I have." It's another of the reasons I love sports. The game is there for all of you to see, the ultimate selfie.

Which leads me to another thought (thanks for coming along)—why are professional sports for women so much less popular than the men's? I admit, I wanted to cover the Final Four, not "the Women's Final Four." I wanted to cover Duke and Kansas, Louisville and Kentucky, not Tennessee and Connecticut women. I was both right and wrong. Men's basketball, absent those two women's programs, had been where the action was for almost fifty years. I only went to WNBA games when either of my friends Donna Orender or Val Ackerman were the commissioners. I did one of the last interviews with the late Pat Summitt of Tennessee, and it made my heart swell with sadness and pride.

She was everything every woman would want to be: tough, original, a fighter, and a friend. She was nearing the end, but she did recall one national championship (she won eight), when the Lady Vols were trailing by ten with eight minutes to go against North Carolina. She gathered her team in the huddle and said, "We are not going home without a national championship!" I adored her, as did so many of her players and fans. She managed to raise a terrific son, Tyler, while making homemade ice cream and shooting hoops with him in the backyard. Geno Auriemma is close to the same at UConn, but I admit I knew Jim Calhoun much better. Auriemma, like many people, would quote John Wooden's "Pyramid of Success," adding that Wooden had Lew Alcindor, Bill Walton, and Gail Goodrich, while she had Diana Taurasi, Maya Moore, and Breanna Stewart.

Most of us know names like Wooden, even sixty years later, but many Americans would have no idea who Auriemma is talking about. And why is that? All coaches want their players to live up to their potential, to practice like they play, to contribute and not to slack off. So why do we pay attention to the men and not the women? I have a theory; tell me what you think. I believe Americans love a big event; it's why we know Simone Biles but have not seen another gymnastics event outside the Olympics. It's why we know Hope Solo, but have never been to a women's professional soccer game. I went to one in Boca Raton, Florida, when she was the goalie and there were maybe five hundred people at the game—and this was

With Kevin Costner at his fortieth birthday party in Los Angeles in 1995. I bought him a Green Bay cheesehead for a present.

after the World Championships. I also think we'll follow women's individual sports—tennis or golf—but not team sports. Admittedly, it's a circular chain of popularity. The media follows where the sponsors and the investors go; the advertisers go where the popularity is. The Women's Sports Foundation estimated that women receive only 7 percent of media coverage and less than 1 percent of commercial sponsorship. The PGA offers more than $250 million in prize money; the LPGA, less than $50 million.

There are small steps of hope for women. LaChina Robinson from ESPN was asked if she wanted to cover the NBA and the former basketball player declined, telling Lauren Gentile (the senior VP of ESPN's women's initiatives) and producer Carol Stiff that she preferred to cover the women's NCAA and WNBA. And after the 2012 Olympics in London, more than 500,000 women took up some form of sport. Are we going back to the future? In 1908, Marie Marvingt was denied the right to ride in the Tour de France. She did anyway and of the 115 people who started the 4,500-kilometer race, 37 managed to complete it: 36 men and 1 woman.

BEARS 2005

F GAME ONE

isser
orts

CBS SPORTS

10819

PRESS BOX

PACKERS

LESLEY
S SPORTS

DIVISIO

NFL

PRESS BOX

LESLEY VISSER
CBS SPORTS

SUNDAY NOVEM

VS

PRESS BOX

GAME 6

LAMBEAU FIELD

1957-2007

6500

Sept 31 2005

AUTHORIZED BY

AUTOGRAPHS

AFFILIATION

NAME

CBS

CHAPTER 7

My four favorite coaches of all time are Rick Majerus, Rick Pitino, Jim Valvano, and Bill Parcells. Majerus and Valvano died too young, Parcells retired, and Pitino won two championships at different schools before being put on administrative leave from Louisville (in his words "effectively fired") for a pay-for-play scandal in 2017, about which he declared his innocence. My favorite NFL player was Lawrence Taylor, my favorite college player was Chris Mullin, and my favorite owners are Jerry Jones and Robert Kraft. Yes, Jerry Jones! I think he is a scream. He once told me that when he took his then-girlfriend Jean (now wife) to the Arkansas State Fair in the late 1950s and couldn't knock down the Coke bottles to win her a bear, he went behind the stage and *bought* a bear from the carnival barker! I had huge admiration for Giants owner Wellington Mara (he once had a Mass said for me when I broke my hip) and for gentleman owner Art Rooney. But Jones made me laugh and Kraft gave me all my breaks. When people asked about the locker room, I told them that Robert Kraft was the first one to let me in. Everyone assumed I meant the Patriots, but I didn't. I meant the 1976 Boston Lobsters—a World Tennis team that Kraft owned and that I covered for the *Globe*.

My access to the Lobsters' locker room came in the middle of a wild scene at BU's Walter Brown Arena, with Ion Țiriac as the player-coach followed by the great Roy Emerson and the newly defected Martina Navratilova as the star. Țiriac smoked in the locker room and didn't care who else was there. He was an original—the richest man in Romania (business, insurance, car dealerships) with a wild head of hair and a bowlegged walk. Never one to smile, he was sort of a tennis Bill Belichick, brilliant but surly and slow to laugh. A natural athlete, Țiriac had been a member of the Romanian ice hockey team that competed in the 1964 Olympics in Innsbruck, and he won the French Open tennis doubles with fellow crazy Ilie Năstase. Țiriac said he came to Boston because "the people there were civilized and I got $50 a week under the table."

Bob Kraft didn't even own the Patriots then. The team was owned by businessman Billy Sullivan, a rascal himself, who finally sold the team to Victor Kiam in 1988. By then, I had covered the NFL for more than thirteen years. Many people think women started reporting on the NFL when Lisa Olson was bullied by the Patriots, but that was 1990. Women had been covering the NFL for years. Commissioner Pete Rozelle, followed by Paul Tagliabue, started opening the locker rooms to women in 1982. Of course, it was controversial, but the locker room was the place of business after a game. It's where the stories were. The players could get dressed or cover up if they wanted to. It wasn't sexy. Players were tired and hurt and wanted to go home. The reporters did, too.

Of course I had humiliating moments—who didn't? I remember once, covering the NBA playoffs in 1982, Bob

Ryan and I were sent to Game 3 of the Celtics–Bullets Eastern Conference series in Washington. I had always loved Kentucky guards, back to Louie Dampier, through Kevin Grevey and Kyle Macy. Grevey was playing for the Bullets when they lost Game 3. After the game, Bob Ryan went to the Celtics' winning locker room and I went to the Bullets'. I marched in with the pack of reporters and Grevey saw me. "Oh, God," he said. "No one told us there'd be a fucking broad in here." I turned deep purple and walked over to the only person I saw, some bench warmer who never played and was sitting by himself. After a few minutes, Grevey walked over and apologized, offering to buy me dinner, saying his mother didn't raise him to treat women like that. We've been friends ever since, but at the time I felt lower than a fish on a hook.

It was one moment I wish I'd had Rick Majerus by my side. He was so honorable, so decent, that he would have taken care of it before my face colored red. One time at the Final Four, when one of his players from Utah, Britton Johnsen, was accused of hurling an ethnic slur at Makhtar N'Diaye, an opposing player from North Carolina, Rick stood at the postgame podium and said, "If this is true, I will resign right now." N'Diaye said that maybe he'd misunderstood, and the moment passed.

That's the kind of person Rick was. His father, a union organizer from Sheboygan, Wisconsin, had taken him to civil rights marches in the South. Rick was the only coach I knew who read the *New York Times* every day. He loved to argue philosophy or the in-bounds pass, both with equal enthusiasm. Rick was the guy on the play-ground who was never good enough to get in the game,

With Marquette, Utah, and St. Louis basketball coach Rick Majerus and fellow CBS broadcaster Pat O'Brien at the 1998 Final Four in San Antonio

the sophomore who got cut from his high school team. One time, at Marquette, sitting on the bench for the great Al McGuire, Rick stormed into the coach's office demanding to know why he didn't play ahead of that kid Allie, whom Rick thought he was much better than.

McGuire looked at him, disgusted. "Because your last name isn't McGuire," he said.

I had a great time with Majerus. Terribly overweight, he wanted us to do a TV show called *10*, where I would be the 1 and he would be the 0. He loved going to dinner with me, because he could eat all of his food and half of mine. One time, we drove hundreds of miles to a trailer in El Paso, Texas, where Don "The Bear" Haskins lived with

With Coach Rick Majerus at the 1991 Kentucky Derby

his wife Mary, because Rick said Haskins—who famously coached Texas Western to the NCAA Championship over Kentucky in 1966—was an original and I should meet him. Majerus called Haskins the "John Wayne" of coaching—a fierce competitor who ate and drank and laughed in a larger-than-life cowboy style. I remember Haskins told stories of growing up in Enid, Oklahoma, where one of the water fountains was marked "Colored," and that the only reason he agreed to do a cameo role (as a gas station attendant) in *Glory Road,* Jerry Bruckheimer's brilliant movie about the '66 title game, was that it was important for society to record that an all-black team beat an all-white one. Haskins didn't care about color, he cared about life.

Majerus had been a student, a "player," an assistant coach, and a head coach at Marquette and was on the bench when Al McGuire and the Warriors won the 1977 national title. I wish I knew McGuire better. I remember getting T-shirts for my friends one Christmas in the seventies with McGuire's famous slogan "Life is seashells and balloons, bare feet and wet grass," and I had the honor of working some games with him in the 1990s. At dinner, McGuire would make you introduce yourself to the waiter, "who's just as important as you are." In truth, I think he intimidated me, but I respected everything about him. He once said of Kentucky, "They were there before you, they are there during you, and they will be there after you." He called life how he saw it, and Majerus was blessed to have a lifelong relationship with the quirky coach. Unfortunately, Majerus lost to Rick Pitino and Kentucky in the title game. I used to say there were two things Majerus couldn't beat—saturated fat and Rick Pitino.

Not that Majerus wasn't quirky himself. In all his fifteen years at Utah, he lived in a hotel. I used to say that they'd put a rope around the maid every afternoon and drag her out. Majerus's room was a mess, cold food and half-opened boxes everywhere in sight. I used to hold my nose and go into his room—sneakers and shorts and towels all over the floor. Majerus was famous for doing everything naked, but, thank heavens, he didn't do that around me. One time he invited me to Michael Jordan's "Flight School" in Las Vegas, where Majerus was one of the coaches. At night, he'd order all kinds of appetizers and fall asleep on my shoulder while watching TV. How romantic.

Rick said that in many ways, he was just like me. He worried about his diet. He worried about his mom. He tried to exercise. His final job was St. Louis, where he led the Billikens to a 10–1 start and won his 500th game. From his earliest memories, he was a coach, "putting the pieces together." Here's one story that sums up his connection with people. When Doc Rivers was a high school great, Louisville had Muhammad Ali call to recruit the Chicago legend to play with the Cardinals. Rivers instead went to Marquette—such was the influence of Rick Majerus, who gave him the nickname "Doc" in honor of Julius Erving. Rick's book, with Gene Wojciechowski, was called *My Life on a Napkin*, and it was perfect for Rick, who was always taking notes from working with McGuire or Don Nelson or Del Harris. His wit was legendary. One time, when we were driving too fast, he looked over at me and said, "Don't worry, I'm your airbag."

Bill Parcells was the opposite of Majerus: sly, confrontational, defensive. I loved Parcells; he always grabbed the higher ground. In my first TV interview with him, I was understandably nervous. In the middle of the interview, he leaned over quietly and said to me, "How much would it cost to keep you?"

I was thrown off, unnerved. I stammered, "Well, DeBartolo money," referring to the billionaire owner of the San Francisco 49ers. He sat back and laughed, "Don't flatter yourself." That was Bill Parcells.

I run from confrontation. Parcells embraced it. He saw it as a way to get straight with people. It's not a coincidence that his favorite people were Al Davis and Lawrence Taylor and Bob Knight. He went salmon fishing with Ted Williams and to the Kentucky Derby with Wayne Lukas, all champions. Parcells thought it best to be blunt, to tell a player or a reporter or an assistant coach exactly where that person could be better. It's why his greatest line is so often quoted: "You are what your record says you are." Period. Parcells didn't use humor, he used philosophy—to win games you have to win games. Be a smart team, be well conditioned, be a team with pride. Parcells understood trial and error, but *your* job was to cut down on the errors. He said he was no psychologist, but he really was, which is why the bad boys—from LT to Bryan Cox—loved the guy. I don't think I could have played for Knight, but I would have loved to have played for Parcells.

The first time I ever saw Jim Valvano, who would become such a part of my life, the scene was unforgettable. Do you remember the song "Ain't No Stopping Us Now" by McFadden & Whitehead? In 1979, it was playing on a loudspeaker (there were no sound systems in gyms back then) at an event called "The Boston Shootout."

It was held every year for great high school basketball players from around the country. At the end of the game, when the music stopped, Coach Valvano went over to two of the nationally known players, Dereck Whittenburg and Sidney Lowe from DeMatha Catholic High School in Washington. Jim stuck his hand out and said, "Hi, I'm Jim Valvano, Iona College."

Confused, the two players looked at each other and said, "Wow, this guy owns a college? We better go with him."

And they did, to NC State, where Valvano had begun coaching and the Wolfpack beat Houston for the national title in 1983. Valvano was diagnosed with bone cancer in June of 1992, gave his famous ESPY speech in March of '93, and died almost two months later. He left us with much laughter, a foundation, and memories to last a lifetime. His motto, which he lived by, was, "If you can think, laugh, and cry, you've had a pretty full day."

I've been on the board of the V Foundation for Cancer Research for more than twenty years and I know that Jim Valvano could have been a professional comedian. He was a riot, in addition to being a fantastic coach. The guy majored in English at Rutgers and we would talk Shakespeare as much as we talked Dean Smith's four-corner offense. I once took a two-week road trip with Valvano when he was recruiting for NC State. We'd finish the dinner, after he'd smiled and posed for a thousand pictures. Then we'd get in the van, headed for the next small town. "Wasn't that the absolute worst chicken you ever ate in your life?" he'd ask, speaking to no one in particular. This was a guy who grew up eating great Italian dinners in New York. When Jim got sick—the cancer that was never discovered or named—I wrote him a note, "You'll always be the best white dancer I've ever known."

He wrote me back: "F— you—that's like calling me the world's tallest dwarf!"

We give 100 percent of every dollar we raise for cancer research. Jim insisted on it.

I owe my career to four people—Vince Doria, Ted Shaker, Les Moonves, and Sean McManus—but honestly, there's a fifth, the second love of my life, Pitino. I promise his wife Joanne will understand. As I mentioned, we were kids together. In 1978, at Boston University, Pitino and I would count the people in the stands.

"Forty-nine, fifty, fifty-one—"

"No, Rick," I'd say, "that guy went out to get popcorn, we already counted him."

Rick was able to take chances, trying a press here or an offense there and was able to try a different approach here or an anecdote there.

We grew up together. Then Pitino got great, and he kept getting better. After seven Final Fours (three each at Louisville and Kentucky, one at Providence), I told him I couldn't keep changing T-shirts. A six-foot guard from Long Island who kept changing his methodology to stay ahead of the pack, his approach to success has been to outwork everyone. What I love about Rick is that I've never known him to sell something as a gimmick—he truly embraced the three-point shot—and he really tells a player what his chances of playing are. When you've taken three programs to the Final Four—winning two titles, with Kentucky in 1996 and Louisville in 2013—you're either the greatest overachiever or one of the most

Interviewing Coach Rick Pitino after the championship 2013 Final Four game in Atlanta.

brilliant coaches. I've read all his books; the best is the *The One-Day Contract*. Rick Pitino, my buddy from BU, becomes your coach and tells you how to add value to every day—how you can, just for today, make a deal with yourself that you will be your best. Rick is my ultimate gut check; he always has been.

At the 2010 Kentucky Derby, when Rick introduced me to Bob, I had been in the press room where my friend Jeff DeForrest, a South Florida radio legend, had been bothering me about getting into the big-time "Gold Room" at Churchill Downs. My pal Victoria has controlled the Gold Room for decades, and she finally took pity on DeForrest (whose nose was pressed up against the glass door like

In front of the twin spires at the 2009 Kentucky Derby

a dog) and let him in, but I was so appalled at the way he begged that I left to go find Pitino on Millionaire's Row, where the introduction to Bob happened. In my heart, I believe Pitino knew nothing of the sex scandal in Minardi Hall (named after his best friend and brother-in-law, Billy Minardi) in 2016, where one of his staff members was paying for strippers. I believe that Rick was heartbroken. He's been a coach for more than forty years, a Hall of Famer, and he knows how to get people to work for the common good, to overachieve and to own the consequences. I've been at his fortieth birthday party, his fiftieth, and his sixtieth, and he's had the same friends, the same people, and the same music. His methods of friendship and coaching are both winning and proven.

I was as surprised as anyone when he got a tattoo of a capital "L" over his left shoulder after Louisville won the national championship in 2013. He'd promised his team, and they offered tattoo suggestions, like Mike Tyson's facial tattoo or the Chinese symbol for a redbird. I'd just about gotten used to that horrible white suit Rick drags out every year, but a sixty-year-old man with a tattoo? "It was bad," said Pitino, "but it didn't hurt as much as kidney stones."

One man I worked with in television was unlike any other. I thought Frank Gifford was an American James Bond. He had the résumé that young women, especially

With Frank Gifford while covering the World Skiing Championship in Sierra Nevada, Spain, in 1999

young football fans, dreamed about—thirteen years with the New York Giants as the glamour halfback. He was out of USC and movie-star handsome, and I knew his whole story—how he'd moved more than thirty times because his father had been an oil-rigger. After Frank retired from the NFL in 1964, he went into broadcasting. I got to work with him one year on *Monday Night Football* and many days or nights in other sports. My favorite memory was in Sierra Nevada, Spain, for the World Skiing Championships in the late 1990s. Because the sun was so strong and melted the mountain runs, the skiing would be over by noon, and we would retire to a chalet and drink white wine.

Gifford would talk about the old days of the NFL, including the vicious hit from Philadelphia linebacker Chuck Bednarik, the one that forced Gifford to miss the '61 season. But he also talked about how much fun it was to line up at defensive back—people don't remember that he made eight Pro Bowls at three different positions. That spring, covering skiing in southern Spain (where you can see Morocco from the top of the mountain), we would drive into historic Granada and see the famous all-white Andalusian horses perform, then we'd drive through the fields of sunflowers all the way to the Costa del Sol. It was magical.

My worst experience with Frank Gifford was flying home to New York from a Pro Bowl in Honolulu. I thought, "Great, I get Frank for nine hours and I can hear every story of the old NFL." But then Richard Simmons, that exercise guy in the shorts and a tank top, happened to be in the row in front of us, and he hung—for *nine* hours—over the back of the seat, flirting with Frank.

CHAPTER 8

In addition to my favorite coaches, three other sports leaders—one a baseball manager, and two NFL coaches— have made a huge impression on me, both for their stories and their strength. The first is former manager Joe Torre, who grew up with four brothers and sisters in Marine Park, Brooklyn. He lived in a tidy row house on T Street, where his father was a New York City cop and his mother was a housewife. But inside the small house was a cauldron of rage, a nightly repeat of verbal and emotional abuse. From 1940 until 1995, Joe Torre never admitted the drama that went on behind the pretty lace curtains, but the famously serene man who won four World Series with the New York Yankees, who was there when Don Larsen pitched his perfect game against the Dodgers in 1956, and who became baseball's winningest manager in postseason history—is the man who finally acknowledged the abuse his father Joseph unleashed on his beloved mother Margaret. Hall of Famer Joe Torre, who made the journey from being a terrified child hiding behind a couch in Brooklyn to a plaque in Cooperstown, told me his story of joy and redemption, of winning and losing, of laughter and loss, and about his foundation, Safe At Home, dedicated to young people who have nowhere to go and who witness bullying or worse inside their own homes.

Joe Torre got a hit in his first major-league at-bat. "I was only twenty years old, but I can still feel that person inside me," said Torre, settling in for one of his well-known musings about life and baseball. "The first-place Pittsburgh Pirates were facing us in County Stadium [Torre was a rookie with the Milwaukee Braves]. It was the bottom of the eighth—our manager, Chuck Dressen, decided to put me in as a pinch hitter. The first pitch from Harvey Haddix came in and I didn't swing, but I said to myself, 'Wow, I think I can hit that.' The next pitch, I got a base hit up the middle."

That was late September of 1960, the first of his 2,342 hits over an eighteen-year career as a catcher, first baseman, and third baseman with three teams, the Braves (later Atlanta), the St. Louis Cardinals, and the New York Mets. Although he was a nine-time All Star and the '71 National League MVP, Torre never got to postseason play. That glory would come as a manager, with Yankee titles in '96, '98, '99, and 2000. Ah, those were the years. Joe and his wife Ali, the beauty he found reading a book in a bar in Cincinnati ten years before, lived in Westchester and owned the town. Torre's favorite pregame meal (frittata or whole wheat pasta) would be waiting for him every day at Trattoria Vivolo in Harrison, NY, and the family would gather after games at places like Ponte's downtown (where they'd had their honeymoon meal in 1987) or Elia's on Manhattan's Upper East Side ("I love the fish," said Torre, "and since my prostate cancer in 1999, the chef takes care of me"). There was always a table for them at Primola's, also on Second Avenue, and another one at Il Pastaio in Beverly Hills, especially when Joe was managing the Dodgers from 2008 to 2010.

"I do eat other things besides Italian," said Torre, now chief baseball officer for Major League Baseball, "but I'm just an old dog when it comes to food. I did try wheatgrass once in L.A., but it, ahh, wasn't for me."

Living in Westchester, managing the Yankees for twelve years, was the longest Torre ever lived in one place since childhood. He was able to completely settle in, taking his daughter Andrea trick-or-treating (being mindful to cover his face—one time as the Grim Reaper—so as not to invite long discussions about moving the runner over or managing the bullpen). He loved the job and the job loved him. Derek Jeter often said, "Mr. T is like a second father to me," and Jorge Posada added, "When anyone was struggling, he gave you confidence." Tino Martinez was down on himself and went into Torre's office. "He gave me a cigar, told me that I knew how to play the game, and ordered me to get a good Italian meal," said Martinez. "He never embarrassed you and he never quit on you."

Before Ali, Torre was married twice, in 1963 to Jackie, and in 1968 to Dani. Both earlier marriages were struggles ("I only cared about baseball," he said), and he also struggled to know his adult children, Michael, Lauren, and Christine. Torre had been deeply scarred by the abuse he had witnessed as the youngest of five children. "My father, Joseph, would make my mother get up in the middle of the night to cook for his friends. If he didn't like the food, he would throw it against the wall," Torre said. Although Joe was not physically abused himself, he grew up in fear, panicked to see his father's car in the driveway. Witnessing domestic abuse and feeling helpless to stop it, Joe said he grew up feeling worthless and alone. His cherished older brother, Frank, who'd signed a major league contract with the Boston Braves in 1953, was eight years older and living away. It wasn't until 1995, when Ali encouraged Joe to attend a seminar on life skills, that Torre's feelings came flooding out.

"Ali always made me feel comfortable," said Torre about the much younger woman he met at Stouffer's in Cincinnati the day after a game in 1986. "Although she grew up in a huge family, no one ever doubted the love. I learned so much from her. She basically gave me freedom."

In 2002, with Ali's love and support, Joe started the Safe At Home Foundation. He is the chairman, she is the president. The organization, whose annual gala in New York raises almost $1 million a year with people like Jon Bon Jovi or Paul Simon or James Taylor giving an intimate concert for free, has a mission to tell the children of domestic violence that it's not their fault. Ali and Joe Torre want to educate children about the issues of violence and also give them a place to go. Through more than a dozen safe havens called Margaret's Place (named after Joe's mother), Safe At Home provides protected healing rooms, with everything from counseling to computers to educational opportunities.

"It's for children who witness or experience abuse; it's also about their self-image," said Ali. "Young women get a message in this country that they have to look a certain way—it's constantly reinforced through images twenty-four hours a day. We don't want young girls to think they have to be somebody for somebody else. We want all children to be healthy."

Alice Wolterman Torre grew up among fifteen brothers and sisters in a small town outside of Cincinnati. She liked baseball, went to a few games at Crosley Field (home of the Reds from 1912–1970), but "mostly wanted to go someplace different than the Midwest." When she turned eighteen, she told her mother, "I was buying a one-way ticket to Hawaii, and I did." Always fearless, Ali loved anything physical, from golf to tennis, to skiing and hiking. "I tell Joe that I want to see every national park," said Ali, "and I don't mean Fenway!" While their travels have not taken them to Europe nearly enough—"I want to see Wimbledon in person," she said—one of Joe's proudest moments came in December of 2005 when he carried the Olympic torch relay to the foot of the Ponte Vecchio in Florence in preparation for the Winter Games in Torino, Italy.

"We want to travel more," said Ali. "We've lived more places than many people get to experience—New York, Los Angeles, St. Louis, Atlanta, and Cincinnati—but there is so much we want to do. Our daughter, Andrea, is headed for NYU; she's wanted to be a performer since she was a child."

In Los Angeles, Joe's been willing to experiment. He took yoga classes—"I'm not really into eighteen different positions for my arms and legs, but I finally got that 'downward dog.'" He went surfing, complete with skintight wetsuit and Dodger cap, and has made many trips to the famous tracks around Hollywood. After being introduced to thoroughbred racing in the mid-nineties by his longtime assistant coach and good friend Don Zimmer, Torre took to the sport like horses to hay. He's been the owner, or part owner, of such horses as Sis City, winner of the Ashland Stakes at Keeneland, the filly who finished fourth at the Kentucky Oaks. He won the first leg of the Canadian Triple Crown with Wild Desert, and he's had the favorite, Game On Dude, in the Breeders' Cup Classic. His stable is called Diamond Pride.

"Don Zimmer convinced me to put up $300 almost twenty years ago," said Torre, whose Game On Dude has been ridden by Hall of Fame jockey Mike Smith and trained by Hall of Famer Bob Baffert. "I've never been the same since. I love the game, love everything about horse racing. But after my family, Safe At Home is at the top of my list. I know the program works; I've seen kids recover. People in this country say, 'Well, it's not really my business.' But you know what? It is your business."

The seventy-six-year-old Torre was inducted in Cooperstown along with his great friends Tony La Russa and Bobby Cox. The three legendary managers traded stories and toasts, and talked about the dreams and dances they have shared. The most important manager in the history of the iconic Yankees, who managed fabled victories with thoroughbred players named Jeter and Rivera, Williams, Pettitte, and Posada, also lived through the wild collapse against the Red Sox in 2004. But those Yankee teams, like Torre himself, have been both popular and successful. In his position with Major League Baseball, Torre is asked constantly about instant replay, home plate collisions, and the global game. But he will take more than a few moments to understand what has happened to him personally. He was not a fan of Donald Trump's campaign, although he enjoyed playing golf with the president-elect. Torre told me he thought Trump's campaign was disrespectful to both women and children, and that those topics aren't specific to Democrats or Republicans.

With his patient demeanor and decades-long perspective, Torre managed five major league clubs (the Mets, Braves, Cardinals, Yankees, and Dodgers), and spent another five years as a broadcaster. With a love of green tea and pink bubblegum, in addition to adoring his wife and good red wine, Torre is the only manager to have more than two thousand hits as a player and more than two thousand wins from the dugout. Even though people told him he'd most surely end up in Cooperstown, he said that Hall of Fame call he got still hit him like a "sledgehammer."

"It was about three thousand miles from T Street in Brooklyn to my home in Los Angeles," said Torre, "but emotionally, not so far."

CHAPTER 9

Another coach who made a great impression on me was Bill Walsh of the San Francisco 49ers. Yes, he missed out on drafting Joe Montana early, and yes, he agreed to start an aging O. J. Simpson to sell tickets, but even his struggling teams showed signs of improvement. I only watched from afar in the late 1970s, when Walsh sent assistant coach Sam Wyche to work out three players before the 1979 draft—quarterback Phil Simms, receiver James Owens from UCLA, and quarterback Steve Dills from Stanford. Walsh told Wyche to find someone to throw to Owens. Wyche went back to Walsh and told him he had to take a look at this kid who threw to Owens, Joe Montana out of Notre Dame.

The 49ers had the top pick in 1979 (after a disastrous 2–14 season in 1978, they traded away the number one pick for O. J. Simpson). The 49ers used their first pick of the second round on Owens and took Montana with the third pick of the third round. Both Montana and Walsh had the good fortune to be backed by owner Eddie DeBartolo, the kindly owner who loved his players, won five Super Bowls, and is now in the Pro Football Hall of Fame. He was the most competitive owner in any sport, but one who respected his players and expected greatness

With hall of famer Ed DeBartolo, former owner of the world
championship San Francisco 49ers, and ESPN's Sal Paolantonio

from everyone in the organization. The first time I met
him was in the mid-seventies when the *Boston Globe*
sent me to Youngstown, Ohio, to do a story on Eddie's
father. After the interview, Eddie and his lifelong friend
Carmen Policy took me out on the town and flew me back
to Boston on the DeBartolo jet. They also had someone
return my rental car to Pittsburgh. When DeBartolo got
together with Walsh, there was no stopping them; they
drafted Montana and traded for Steve Young. At one
point in the NFL, twenty of the thirty-two head coaches
had trained under Bill Walsh or were in his coaching tree.

Walsh was a thinking man's head coach. I remember
a friend of mine named Dr. John Murray, a sports

psychologist, said you could predict how certain people would react in certain situations by applying a mental performance index. Walsh always came out on top, because his mind, his imagination, was always engaged. He had a goal and a fierce drive. The first conversation I had with Bill Walsh was in 1983. I was asking about his innovative offense, but he wanted to talk about Muhammad Ali. I'd done one or two interviews with Ali, and Walsh wanted to know everything even though he'd been an expert boxing observer himself. He asked me where I thought Ali's skills came from, what was his motivation. Walsh wanted to know how Ali sustained his excellence over so many years, and the source of his mental stamina. An amateur boxer himself, Walsh wanted to know how he could apply the answers to his football team.

Walsh had read everything about Ali, and what intrigued him the most was that despite Ali's ferociousness, the boxer also had an element of finesse. Walsh wanted to implement that style with his 49ers; the appearance of intellect over muscle. With his white hair and immaculate presentation, Walsh seemed less savage than he really was, but players like Ronnie Lott proved him different. When Lott had the tip of his injured finger cut off to stay in the game, Walsh thought nothing of it— he was both tough and no-nonsense, cerebral and calm.

In 1953, Walsh was a 190-pound boxer who won his college tournament at San Jose State. Players recall him shadow-boxing on the sidelines after 49er practices. The great center Randy Cross once told me that Walsh liked "both the artistic and the violent side of football." Walsh enjoyed being known as a complicated man—well read and thoughtful, but he also put a sign in the 49er locker room that read, "I Will Not Be Out Hit at ANY Time This Season." Walsh was a coach, a teacher, and skilled in the art of combat.

His motivation didn't come through intimidation, like so many of today's coaches. To drive his players, he used attention to detail and expectation of self-awareness. Jerry Rice once told me, "He was *relentless* with us." Widely regarded as the greatest receiver ever to play the game, Rice recalled that, "One game I had twelve receptions, three touchdowns, and two hundred yards, and Bill called me into his office." Walsh didn't meet with Rice to congratulate him; he told Rice the 49ers needed more. Walsh's longtime assistant Mike Holmgren, who went on to win a Super Bowl with the Green Bay Packers, once said, "While the rest of us were pounding an anvil, he was painting a picture."

Walsh wanted an offense that flowed, that moved down the field in an orderly and precise manner. With Joe Montana, he had just the quarterback to do it. It was artistry, football on little cat's feet. And, of course, "Joe Cool" led the perfect offense of short, surgical passes that controlled a game. In ten years, Walsh led the 49ers to three Super Bowl wins and six division crowns, and put together a team that won two more Super Bowls under George Seifert. I covered most of those games, celebrating afterwards with Eddie DeBartolo and his family, while complaining how crummy and wet Candlestick Park was in the winter.

Walsh was born in 1931 in Los Angeles, the son of an auto repair shop worker who moved his family up to San Francisco in the 1940s. Bill was a wide receiver at San Jose State and went on to earn a master's degree with the thesis, "Defending the Spread-T Offense." In 1960, Marv Levy, who'd earned his master's at Harvard, hired Walsh as an assistant at Cal-Berkeley. Walsh became a fixture in the Bay Area, coaching at both Cal and Stanford. He even did a stint with the Oakland Raiders while he and his wife Geri lived in an apartment in San Jose. When the expansion-team Cincinnati Bengals were looking for an offensive assistant, Walsh was hired as the receivers coach under the legendary Paul Brown.

The now storied career of Bill Walsh, who's often forgotten when people mention Lombardi or Shula, Belichick or Parcells, Halas or Paul Brown himself, had its modest roots with the Cincinnati Bengals. Those who remember Brown know that he was a football and cultural warrior. In the mid-1940s, he modernized the game and brought in players from all walks of life—sons of Italy and Ireland, Poland and Hungary. Many of the players were just home from World War II, so when Brown stressed discipline, the young men completely understood. Walsh learned from Brown how to be presentable—players were expected to sit up straight and wear white shirts at dinner, and to motivate themselves.

Wearing a topcoat and a fedora, Brown was a pioneer, inventing the two-guard system where he would shuttle in offensive linemen (the great Chuck Noll was one of them) to change a play. In addition, Brown stressed scouting. His

Cleveland Browns, using this approach and quarterback Otto Graham, completely dominated the old All-America Football Conference. When both Brown and Walsh were with Cincinnati, they came up with the West Coast Offense, based on perfectly timed short passes, where a receiver ran to a specific spot. Brown called it his "nickel and dime" offense, but eventually Ken Anderson and Isaac Curtis became the prototypes for Joe Montana and Jerry Rice.

Walsh began "scripting" his plays, unusual at the time. Paul Brown would intensely ask Walsh what he thought the opening plays should be and Walsh was ready for the inquisition. Eventually, Walsh would have ten or twelve plays laid out, and they gave the team time to rehearse exactly what the players were expected to do. Walsh said it even gave him a better night's rest. Brown retired in 1975, when I started covering the NFL, and he gave the head coaching job to Bill Johnson. Bill Walsh was crushed; he left, taking his West Coast Offense to the San Diego Chargers, and went on to beat the Bengals in two Super Bowls. Walsh said he had a quiet fury, and a drive born of not being the first pick. Roger Craig, the great 49ers running back, once told me that "Bill Walsh had a charisma, a kind of glow. I guess you could call it a champion's glow."

And it was true. Walsh brought what he'd learned from both Paul Brown and Sid Gillman to Stanford, where he used the pass to set up the run. Eddie DeBartolo noticed the middle-aged coach and hired him for the 49ers when both were at the Doral Hotel in Miami, after the Niners had suffered through another horrible season in 1978. Walsh was finally ready, even though he'd been passed over for NFL head jobs until he was forty-seven years old. With DeBartolo, he drafted a skinny quarterback out of Notre Dame in 1979, Joe Montana, and traded for another future Hall of Famer, Steve Young, in 1987. Walsh and DeBartolo didn't want to browbeat their players; they wanted to treat them intelligently.

Walsh went at the job with a quiet vengeance, using many boxing metaphors to motivate his players. Instead of screaming or whipping them into submission, Walsh would say, "Beat your opponent to the punch," or, "The first step is the quickest." Walsh wrote a book with well-known beat writer Glenn Dickey, in which he declared, "Our team will mentally explode off the line." That quickness, both mental and physical, became the team's trademark. I was there when receiver Dwight Clark went behind Everson Walls in the end zone of the 1981 NFC Championship Game to beat the Cowboys, 28–27. It was the final drive of the game, which Montana had started on his own 11-yard line. The winning pass, known as Sprint Right Option, launched the legacy that the 49ers enjoyed that decade and beyond. Dwight told me last year that he hears about the play "at least twice a day." And that was more than three decades ago.

Walsh needed a certain type of quarterback, and Montana was it. He once told me that his quarterback had to be a leader, had to throw a catchable ball under pressure, and had to throw with enough velocity that he could eliminate a defender. On the other side, his receivers had requirements, too. They had to be able to jam the defender at the line of scrimmage, be quick (though not necessarily lightning fast), and have soft hands.

Cue the heavenly choir. From a little-known Division I-AA school called Mississippi Valley State, Walsh noticed a receiver named Jerry Rice. The son of a laborer who hauled bricks all day, Rice was raw and precious, a diamond in the rough. In his rookie year, I asked him what he was going to do with his signing bonus. He said he was going to buy "two cars."

"Two cars?" I asked. "What for?"

He looked at me as if I were a fool. "One for heah," he said in his soft Delta accent, "and one for theyah." Oh, of course. Then we both laughed.

Walsh even maneuvered up in the 1985 draft, trading for the Patriots' sixteenth pick overall, even though Rice was considered no better than the fifth best receiver. Walsh didn't want to take a chance. And Rice was everything Walsh needed, with just enough speed to stretch the field, and near-perfect skills to catch the pass. Some now say Rice has been the best player in the history of the NFL.

Walsh knew that success wasn't a matter of desire, but of talent and preparation. He once said he often repeated the legendary John Wooden's motto, "Failure to prepare is preparing to fail." In ten years with the 49ers, Walsh made forty trades, moving up, moving down, taking only those who interested him. He learned his draft strategy from Paul Brown in Cincinnati, and also from Al Davis, his head coach with the Raiders.

I covered one of the 49ers drafts for ESPN and it was a study in organization. The offices were thirty minutes south of Candlestick and on draft day, Walsh sat with eleven of his coaches and six of his scouts in front of a ten-foot blackboard. (Yes, a blackboard—I often laugh with my CBS colleague Amy Trask, who was the CEO of the Oakland Raiders for nearly three decades, about how people had chalk and erasers back then!) Walsh had offensive charts, defensive charts, and position charts all around him, with General Manager John McVay on the phone from draft headquarters in New York. Eddie DeBartolo was on another phone hookup from Youngstown, Ohio. McVay told me Walsh would listen to everyone, then make his pick. "He was never paralyzed or uncertain," he said.

My CBS headshot

Walsh was always teaching, always thinking. He told me once that while coaching at Washington High School in Fremont, California, in 1957, he made the cheerleaders take a class called "Football 101." No concept was too big, no detail too small. And he never looked ruffled, as if trailing by twenty-seven points would mean nothing by the end of the game. In all his years of determination and success, he told me his proudest moment came when coaching the 49ers to the Super Bowl XXIII Championship in 1989. And not even the whole game, just the final drive. Walsh said that all his years of purpose and practice came together in those three minutes and twenty seconds. "Eleven plays," he said, "that made a symphony."

Of course, the 49ers were trailing the Bengals, and I saw Boomer Esiason practicing "I'm going to Disneyland!" with a camera crew as Montana moved the team down the field. Calling his own plays, the 49ers moved as if they were a machine. Montana hit Rice for 17 yards and Roger Craig for another 11. Esiason looked out the corner of his eye and was filled with dread. When Montana rifled the 10-yard winning touchdown to John Taylor with thirty-four seconds left, for the winning score, the Disney people ditched Esiason and went sprinting across the field. Cincinnati failed to move out of their own territory and the 49ers won, 20–16. Rice was named the MVP for his record 215 receiving yards, all on a tender ankle. It cemented the legacy of both the team and their "Professor" coach.

CHAPTER 10

I t wasn't so long ago that Bill Belichick, my third inspira-
tional sports leader, said he could remember every play
of the 1959 Naval Academy team playbook. Belichick
was six years old when his father, Steve, coached at
Annapolis. I challenged him. When he was well into his
sixties, I brought a whiteboard to an interview in Gillette
Stadium with Belichick and his childhood idol, Heisman
Trophy winner Joe Bellino, Naval Academy class of 1960.
I asked Belichick to diagram Bellino's favorite play.

Belichick took the whiteboard and the black marker
and in ten seconds drew up "F 27 Trap," even diagram-
ming it so Bellino scored a touchdown! Belichick handed
it to Bellino, who gave it a thumbs-up as Belichick beamed
as though he were six again.

It's a side of Belichick most people don't see. The man
who mumbles at most questions, who threw away his
Microsoft Surface tablet on the sideline, and who commented on Brady's record-tying 200th win with, "Well,
it's a quarterback's job to win games," is actually a
thinking-man's mush-ball. That's right. He puts the team
first, he honors the traditions of football (learned at the
Naval Academy), and he wants, first and only, for each
player to just "Do Your Job." Belichick is not sentimental

about the ability of players, but he does have a soft spot for those who give their all.

When Belichick gave up his tablet, which the league uses on the sidelines to provide images of players (and which he declared a nightmare), he said, old school, "I'll stick with pictures—there just isn't enough consistency." Ah, consistency, one of Belichick's favorite concepts. In 1975, after he'd been the captain of Wesleyan lacrosse, the Baltimore Colts hired him as a glorified gofer. He had two more stops, Detroit and Denver, while he was mastering the NFL game, then he joined Parcells with the Giants in the 1980s. Parcells, never one to embrace anybody publically, called him Coach Doom and Gloom, but Belichick was an excellent defensive coach.

In 1979, on a windy day in Giants Stadium, the great Will McDonough said to me out the side of his mouth, "Go meet that guy, Bill Belichick, he's going to be great." I hustled across the field and extended my hand. "Hi, I'm Lesley Visser from the *Boston Globe*." He looked at me like I was from Mars. We talked about lacrosse, since I had lived for a while in Easton, Maryland, which is on the Eastern Shore, across from Annapolis, and both are big on lacrosse. It was a natural conversation, not the scripted responses he gives now. I've had many dealings with Bill over the last three decades, pregame, postgame, features, and conversations, and he's been all over the spectrum— friendly, cold, dismissive, and warm. The famed NFL General Manager Ernie Accorsi, who hired Belichick as the head coach of the Cleveland Browns in 1991, once said, "Almost better than anyone, Bill Belichick learned from his mistakes. He learned how to win Super Bowls."

I used to think I knew Bill Belichick (there was a time when we exchanged personal Christmas cards!), and I always flattered myself that I understood him. I had had a private school education at Derby Academy, and he was a product of Phillips Academy in Andover, Massachusetts. Although it might seem unimaginable, I can guarantee there was a time that Belichick said "Yes, Sir" and "No, Sir" and looked people in the eye. In New England, he is considered emotionless and remote. He lives in Hingham and Nantucket, but the way he acts, he could live anywhere. It's not that he doesn't care, it's that he doesn't care if *you* care. After that, he just wins division titles, conference titles, and five Super Bowls. And for that, New England has decided that he has earned their trust.

People who know him well say he actually has a sense of humor, that he jokes and even laughs out loud. In thirty-five years, I've seen this once or twice. Bill is sarcastic, busting players for giving up too much yardage on third down, questioning every player on a specific route, then dressing up for a player's Halloween party. If you love football, if you "Do Your Job," he's fun to play for; if not, you're gone. When I met him in 1979, he was part of the great Ray Perkins's staff. Perkins was a taskmaster—he'd coached at Alabama and learned from the legendary Bear Bryant, but Perkins and I got along great. My original impression was that Belichick was socially awkward (one friend calls him an "epic slog"), but that didn't include his depth, the acumen it took to go to Andover and Wesleyan. And of all the people he could have befriended at Andover, he picked Ernie Adams, a guy with no ego who loved Latin, football, and naval history. I always said that underneath Belichick's boorish behavior is a prep-school guy who knows exactly what is going on.

Yes, Belichick has made some questionable moves—first-round disappointments in Brandon Meriweather and Laurence Maroney, and both the Spygate and Deflategate sagas—but the number of career victories (more than two hundred) and five Super Bowl rings prove that the man is the best among active coaches, actually better than many coaches in the Pro Football Hall of Fame. One interesting aspect of Belichick is how he flipped from being obsessed with defense to being obsessed with offense, how he went from designing low-scoring games to becoming the pass-happy Patriots. The Patriots set the NFL season scoring record in 2007, then led the league again in scoring in 2012, while setting the league record for first downs. Belichick grew to love the no-huddle and rule changes that favored the offense, and he decided that it's better to aim for 45 points a game than 20.

Belichick was a football lifer from the start. Born in Nashville, his father moved around until finally settling in as a scout for the Naval Academy. Steve Belichick would take young Bill, an only child, to practices, and when things got busy, Bill would go by himself to a projector room and break down film. Bill Parcells, his coach from 1983 to 1990, said, "Bill lived this game his whole life. He knew the nuances at a very early age. He likes to portray the image of an outlaw, but he's really just a guy who likes to look at film and diagram plays."

I remember once when I had to do a story on Andre Rison, who played for Belichick with the Cleveland

Browns. Rison's girlfriend at the time was Lisa "Left Eye" Lopes, a member of the group TLC. The Rock and Roll Hall of Fame agreed to close for one hour so Rison and Left Eye could give CBS a tour. I told Andre that he could not be late, and Bill suggested I take Andre's AMEX card and not give it back to him until he was on the steps of the Rock and Roll Hall of Fame. It worked perfectly, and it made me laugh. Even though Belichick had a terrible experience in Cleveland, he surrounded himself with greatness. The assistant coaches with the Browns, among others, were Nick Saban (of Croatian descent, as is Belichick), Jim Schwartz, and Kirk Ferentz. And Belichick outworked them all. God forbid you had family or kids—Bill lived in a rented apartment with a cardboard box as a coffee table. When the assistant coaches didn't break down film exactly as he wanted, he spent countless hours breaking it down with them.

After three years of losing football, Belichick turned it around in 1994, winning eleven games, but Art Modell was at the end of his bank account and was moving the team to Baltimore. I covered the last game in Cleveland in December of 1995, with the 20-degree wind whipping off Lake Erie and people burning stuffed dolls of Modell. But Modell felt he had nowhere to go and no help from the local government. Instead of 80,000 people freezing and cheering at Cleveland Municipal Stadium, there was bitterness and silence, and it took a toll on Belichick. The Browns won the game, but Cleveland had lost six of their last seven games and the city was depressed. I'll never forget Belichick's final press conference, as people taunted, "Bill Must Go." Belichick waited for them to finish, and it was clear he was just as torn as they were. His next few years were rocky, coaching with Parcells for both the New England Patriots and the New York Jets. Wanting to get out from under the enormous shadow of Parcells, he finally bolted back to New England and from there—destiny. Did he make Tom Brady, or did Brady make him? We'll never know, but the culture Belichick created has stood the test of time. Do your job.

CHAPTER 11

In the early 1980s, after John Madden had been out of coaching for nearly five years, I took the train with him to Minnesota. It was Amtrak's "Lake Shore Limited," meaning it stopped in Chicago. John was only forty-four then; he'd coached for ten years with the Oakland Raiders and had a Super Bowl title and an ulcer to show for it. In 1979, he went into broadcasting, but he soon felt crowded at 30,000 feet. With the Raiders charter flights, he would sit in his seat for takeoffs and landings, then he'd get up to talk to coaches and players. But when he became a broadcaster, he had to sit in his seat. He hated it. In the late fall of 1979, he had what he called a "full-blown panic attack" in Tampa, sweating all the way to New Orleans, where he called his wife Virginia (then in Oakland) to come get him by car. That's when he went to Amtrak.

I met him outside his home at the Dakota in New York. His huge apartment was across from where John and Yoko lived, and Madden was there in 1980 when Lennon was shot outside the entrance. We took the train from Penn Station, and I'll never forget the scene. Madden was six foot four, wearing sneakers with untied laces, and he was already famous from the Miller Lite ads. The railroad car we boarded was nearly full except for one seat next to

John. The next guy who got on the train took that seat. John looked at me sideways until the man finally said, "Do you think the Giants have a chance this year?" And so it went at every stop—Syracuse, Cleveland, Toledo, Elkhart, Indiana.

John loved people and they loved him, but he had some rules. "You can never let them buy you a drink," he said, "because then they think they can sit with you and nurse it for three hours." He also had certain favorites in the dining car, which comprised ten small tables with blue paper tablecloths. John loved the short ribs, and was saddened when Amtrak took them off the menu. From then on, he went for the chicken Kiev. Always America's best-known commuter, Madden enjoyed the club car and

In Central Park with friends at midnight as the millennium ended

the endless questions about the Raiders' 32–14 win over the Vikings in Super Bowl XI, which he loved, as he said of the game played at the Rose Bowl, "because it was played on *grass*. Real grass." After a few years of crisscrossing the country by train, he went to the Madden Cruiser.

It began in 1987 when John needed a bus for a photo shoot, so he rented Dolly Parton's tour bus. He loved it and decided to get one of his own. He became a celebrity on wheels, at first with Greyhound—an $800,000 command post called the Madden Cruiser. It was a blast. With two drivers, in the beginning Willie Yarbrough and Dave Hahn, with Joe Mitchell later replacing Hahn, the forty-five-foot luxury coach was a rolling party, filled with friends or players or his agent, Sandy Montag. By the time he retired in 2009, Madden had been through four buses, and during his ten years with Outback Steakhouse and his buddy, CEO Chris Sullivan, Madden had visited more than half of the one thousand Outbacks in America. Madden loved every one of those buses, the E1500 Entertainer made by Motor Coach in Schaumberg, Illinois. When the Madden Cruiser pulled into town, people lined up to see it, like the bus was a celebrity itself.

I remember once in Chicago, I'd ridden with him to do a Bears game at Soldier Field, and the bus was parked down by the Navy Pier. More people oohed and ahhed at the red and white cruiser (later orange and green with an Australian Outback boomerang painted on the side) than they did at the 150-foot Ferris wheel. There was no denying it was impressive. With multiple TVs, cell phones, an enormous bedroom, and complete navigation system, John didn't want for anything. There was a deal to traveling with him on the bus. No complaining, no stopping except for gas, a greasy diner, or a high school game. And no being late. "Wheels up at 10 AM," John would say, and if you weren't outside the Dakota at 9:45, the bus was leaving without you.

Young people might not know him now, but John Madden was a Mark Twain of our time. His observations were original and funny. One time, riding through Iowa, he said, "I don't get it with dark chocolate—it's like they got halfway to milk and quit." Another time, on our way to a 49ers game, he said, "You know, in a hotel, where you sleep by the side of the bed where the phone is? You must never do that, because that's where every business-man sat his ass while he was on the phone." There was no telling what would come out of his mouth. When riding in Nebraska one time, John said, "People in Nebraska weren't just pioneers—they know their Cornhuskers!"

John loved enthusiasm, and he loved learning. He told me once that he came within one degree of getting his PhD (he already had a master's) but that if someone like him could get a PhD, what was it worth? As a teenager, he read everything by John Steinbeck, especially *Travels with Charley*—and that book informed his life. Madden wanted to see America, not just fly over it. He was born in Austin, Minnesota (the home of Spam, as he often reminded me), but he only lived there until he was six. Then his family moved to California, but he never lost his love of people and places. He would watch fishermen in Longboat Key, Florida, or people raking leaves in Green Bay. His favorite Mexican food was a restaurant called Chuy's in Van Horn, Texas, where he'd call ahead of time

Pregame interview with John Madden and Pat Summerall at Super Bowl XXIV

and Mama Chuy would make chicken and beans and rice. He loved ordering off the plastic laminated menu, and he devoured Mama Chuy's homemade tortillas.

When traveling, Madden would sit by the window on the right-hand booth, with a Diet Coke or bottle of water, and watch I-80 in New York disappear into Middle America. When coming from California, he would take Interstate Highway 5 and stop at Wool Growers, a Basque restaurant in Los Banos, where Madden had the pork chops and ice cream. What he'd learned from Steinbeck was just how big America really is, and wherever you are reading this, Madden was right—you shouldn't just go to New York or Chicago or San Francisco or Orlando, you should spend time in the middle. Madden always said that before anyone could be a senator or a president, he or she should travel the country—"How can you represent America if you haven't seen it?" Madden himself had to learn it the hard way. One of his assistants with the Raiders in the mid-1970s was his childhood friend John Robinson. Robinson told John that he had no life other than looking at football tapes or coaching games. Madden told Robinson he was right—and ten years later, after he'd changed his life, we'd stop in a diner in Elko, Nevada, to eat and talk and walk. Madden used to say he slept better on the bus than he did at home.

Madden's life was easy in some respects. He didn't have to drive through rush-hour traffic, he slept through it. He missed most of the people honking and waving at the Madden Cruiser like it was some kind of display at the Smithsonian. He could look out the window at the wide, open spaces and identify a gray burro or a llama or a deer. Then he could drive into the glorious foliage of western Pennsylvania. We would stop in Clarion, Pennsylvania, and eat at Vinny's, where John was treated like a visiting dignitary. Madden went crazy over small places with an Ace Hardware store in the center of town. He would talk to the managers about peg hooks and power tools. One year for Christmas, John gave me the bus as a present on Christmas Eve. I got twenty-five of my girlfriends, and the Madden Cruiser went around to bars in New York. John didn't come with us, but he said if any of these young women couldn't get lucky on Christmas Eve getting off the Madden Cruiser, they might as well move.

He really enjoyed his busman's holiday, taking fifty hours to cross the country, usually on Interstate 10 in the South or Interstate 80 in the North. And he loved discovering new places, like a seafood joint in Mississippi or a new cafe in the Twin Cities. He would stop for a festival or a softball game, and he lived by the Outback motto on the front of the bus, "No Rules, Just Right." By the time we would get back to I-80 headed into New York, John's spirits would fall. He hated the construction and the bumper-to-bumper traffic. He missed eating at Grandpa's Steakhouse in Kearney, Nebraska, or the small Italian place in Reno, Nevada. The only thing that saved his sanity was that he felt America was balanced: "People in big cities didn't want to live on the farms and the people in Kansas don't want to live in New York."

CHAPTER 12

I shouldn't admit it, but I loved having Thanksgiving on the Madden Cruiser. I know my mother and my aunts and my cousins missed me, and I pretended to be blue, but it was great being in either Dallas or Detroit when John had his six-legged turkey and the players would come by after the game for a spread that included green bean casserole, hearty stuffing, cornbread, sautéed carrots, plus my favorite sweet potatoes with brown sugar, marshmallows, cinnamon, and nutmeg. John's two drivers, Dave Hahn and Willie Yarbrough, would hide the pan of sweet potatoes until I got there, in case I had to do a postgame report and the players had wolfed it down.

Traveling in sports for forty years has not only shown me the way America lives; it's taught my taste buds a thing or two. I was a child of simple food: grilled cheese, peanut butter and jelly, Fenway Franks, bologna, and Velveeta. But going to all these great cities showed me just how good food can be. To this day, I still don't cook, but I appreciate regional differences.

I had my first po'boy in New Orleans when I went to an NCAA Regional in Baton Rouge in 1976. I have to say, I didn't really get the po'boy—I can't stand oysters—but the games were fantastic: Indiana, Marquette (Al

McGuire was late for the tip-off), Western Michigan, and Alabama. Bob Knight, of course, won the National Championship that year with one of his greatest teams, and I remember thinking, Wow, Pete Maravich played here in Baton Rouge. I did like eating a muffaletta, which I think was made of pork and olives.

Some twenty-seven years later, CBS sent me to Breaux Bridge, Louisiana, not far from Baton Rouge, to spend the day with Jake Delhomme, quarterback of the Carolina Panthers, shortly before they lost to Tom Brady and the Patriots in the great Super Bowl XXXVIII. It's a pretty part of the country, two hours west of New Orleans, deep in Cajun country. Half the street signs are in French. Jake was 100 percent Cajun, the proud son of Jerry and Marcia Delhomme (French for "of the man") and husband of Keri Melancon, whom he met in seventh grade. There are only seven thousand people in Breaux Bridge, and half of them had "Geaux Jake!" signs planted in their front lawns, like he was running for office. The day I went there, his mother had spent all morning making the famous Cajun delicacy boudin, which is a French euphemism for "disgusting pork liver and heart meat." I told Jake there was no way I could eat that sausage and he said, "My mother spent half the night and all morning making it for you and you will eat it." Ugh. I did, biting into the pork sausage casings while twenty grandchildren were watching, and I pretended to be thankful. What happened to grilled cheese sandwiches?

I took John Madden to the famed Anchor Bar in Buffalo for the first time. It had to be in the late 1980s. I had been there many times before since my college roommate

A 2009 interview with pro golfer Kenny Perry, runner-up at the 2009 Masters Tournament

Jeanne and her husband, Mo, were from Buffalo, but this was John's first time. And he loved it—it's kind of a dive, of course on Main Street, with a menu that asks if you want your wings "mild, medium, hot, or suicidal!" There were all kinds of different sauces, the people loved John, and the bill came to $37. I think John doubled the bill in his tip.

Buffalo also taught me "beef on weck"—not "on a weck" but "on weck." I just remember it had a lot of horse-radish. The classiest sandwich, of course, is the pimento cheese at Augusta, which is only $1.50, but costs thousands more because you have to get to the Masters to be able to buy one. It's a very simple sandwich—tons of cheese, simple white bread, and lots of mayonnaise—and you get to see Phil Mickelson or Jason Day while eating it. It's not much to look at, but the setting is spectacular.

I never knew bratwurst before I started going to Green Bay, but there is no NFL tailgate like the ones at Lambeau Field, where Packers fans put brats on a grill and serve deviled eggs with Wisconsin cheddar cheese and "finger food" that is chicken wrapped in bacon, which ends up mostly bacon. Everyone wears a Packer jersey (number 4, Favre, is still huge, but now there are many, many Aaron Rodgers shirts, along with old Reggie Whites and new Clay Matthews). It seems that all of Oneida Nation is on hand, eating and dancing in the parking lot, no matter what the weather or the temperature.

Kansas City also has great tailgating, and the barbeque is like no other. My favorite is Joe's, which started as a gas station. Joe's brisket sandwich has smoked provolone and fantastic onion rings. And they'll ship! As a native Bostonian, I can tell you there is nothing like a great clam roll—the best fried clams, of course, come from Ipswich, right there fresh from the Great Marsh. Pick any shack in Ipswich. For more than one hundred years, the clams have been the best, even better with coleslaw and onion rings. There are also lobster rolls from Maine to the Cape to the Patriots' parking lot—those tailgates are great, too, with fresh lobster meat and lots of butter. And go heavy on the mayo.

I'd never even heard of a cheesesteak until I started covering games in Philadelphia. Where had I been? The great Philly cheesesteak, from Geno's or Pat's, is heaven on earth. It might be the water or the bread, but the

With Red Sox great Big Papi before throwing out the first pitch in 2015

authentic Philly cheesesteak is chopped steak, caramel-
ized onions, and maybe some peppers, always on an
Italian roll. Heck, it was born in the Italian section of
Philly (Pat's is on the corner of Passyunk and Wharton,
and it's open all the time, so following the Eagles,
Villanova, or any Big 5 or 76ers game, you can always
go there). Some people like to add mushrooms, but I
think they make a cheesesteak mushy.

People in America don't travel enough to Pittsburgh,
but it's a wonderful city. In western Pennsylvania, it's the
junction of three rivers. In the early 1900s, it was one of
America's great industrial cities. What once was a steel
mill town (hence the name of the NFL team, which has

With Hall of Fame Pittsburgh Steelers running back Jerome Bettis on his famous bus in 2001

been in the iconic Rooney family since 1933), Pittsburgh is now a technology center for companies like Google, IBM, and U.S. defense, and has become a global leader in cybersecurity. The dialect takes some getting used to ("yinz" is the equivalent of "y'all"), but the food is fantastic. Because of the blend of immigrants, people eat everything from pierogis to pizza. Don't forget that John Heinz started his ketchup company there in 1869, and the world's first commercial radio station (and eventually one of its first TV stations), KDKA, was started in Pittsburgh in 1920. My favorite sandwiches are from the famous Primanti Brothers restaurant, which began as a lunch cart during the Depression. They cook the meat and cheese fresh on the griddle, and you should ask them to add the hand-cut fries and maybe some coleslaw to the sandwich. It's messy, but who cares?

St. Louis and Milwaukee, like Pittsburgh, are underrated cities, and not just the food. Milwaukee has the Harley-Davidson Museum, a gorgeous art museum, and everything from Serbian sandwiches to bratwurst and salami, plus hundreds of beers on tap. You have to make a picnic from Usinger's (they supplied brats for the 2002 Winter Games) and the Wisconsin Cheese Mart on West Highland, then head for the beautiful water park. Don't forget the Kopp's frozen custard—the late, great coach

With St. Louis Cardinals manager Tony La Russa before throwing a first pitch for the Cardinals in 2007

Rick Majerus, who was from Sheboygan, used to make me go there at least twice a day. Ribs are found everywhere in St. Louis, but you want to go to a place that serves them Memphis style, like Pappy's Smokehouse. The smoker is parked out back. St. Louis is a different animal. There is the glory of the Gateway Arch, and people sometimes eat a vegan breakfast with a sprinkled cupcake. I've been there many times, through the old NFL Cardinals, on the sideline when the Rams finally won a Super Bowl over Tennessee (yes, Dick Vermeil cried), and to basketball games when Majerus was coaching at St. Louis. We Boston Red Sox fans even consider the St. Louis Cardinals our National League team. Manager Tony La Russa once had me throw out a first pitch. Has it landed yet?

Denver is a mile high and fantastic to look at, but the menu is limited, at least for me. These are your choices and if you like them, have at it. Rocky Mountain oysters are everywhere, but the ranchers are partial to game—elk, venison, and antelope. There are a couple of standouts in the beer category. Of course, the great Coors Brewing Company is from nearby Golden, but if you insist on eating and drinking, I suggest a burrito (smothered in hot green chiles—probably taken from the Mexicans who brought it to Denver). Go to a hole-in-the-wall called Chubby's. As for beer, the Falling Rock Tap House claims "No Crap on Tap" (they even charge you $1 for a stupid question), and it's located only half a block from home plate at Coors Field.

Besides the hyperactive bar at the American Airlines Arena and the gastronomic and visual fiesta on South Beach, the best food in Miami is Cuban. Go anywhere in Little Havana, but Versailles is the cultural icon. Go with a group and order vaca frita de pollo, stuffed green plantains, empanada pies, and some authentic Cuban coffee. For a Cuban sandwich on the run, buy it from a food truck. They are everywhere in South Florida, from Hialeah to Wynwood to Haulover Park, but one of the best is owned by the son of NBC sportscaster Andrea Joyce and her legendary broadcaster husband Harry Smith. Jake Smith has a sushi food truck, Myumi, that has lines around the block. Who knew?

San Francisco tailgating is a drag. The food at Candlestick was always below average, the stadium itself was below sea level, and we always stayed in those hotels near Burlingame—miles from downtown. I loved the 49ers—back in 1977, I had to do a story on Eddie DeBartolo Sr. in Youngstown, Ohio, and his son, Hall of Famer Eddie Jr. (a lifelong friend), insisted on flying me back to Boston on the DeBartolo plane. It was just the pilot and me in their huge Citation jet, plus Eddie had stocked it with a pitcher of margaritas and a bowl of M&Ms. No wonder he's so popular. If I were in San Francisco for a baseball Giants game, there was no stopping me from getting lunch at the Tadich Grill, the old seafood restaurant that's been there 170 years. Save room for the Tadich rice custard. Or go to the new Levi's Stadium, where CBS broadcast Super Bowl 50. Here are some of your choices during the game (a mobile app will help you find them): fresh Dungeness crab on sourdough bread, crab fondue, Asian rice bowl, carrot cake, or wines from Napa and Sonoma!

I first started going to Seattle for the Final Four in the 1980s, and everything I'd heard—that it rained all the time and it was miserable—couldn't be further from the truth. I've been there about twenty-five times now and it's always Chamber of Commerce weather: exhilarating sunshine and fresh air. The Kingdome was nothing to look at, built as a multipurpose facility to hold 60,000 people, but I covered all three Final Fours there—victories by Georgetown in 1984 (Patrick Ewing over Hakeem Olajuwon), Michigan over Seton Hall (Rumeal Robinson at the free throw line in the final seconds), and UCLA over Arkansas (the first Bruin win without John Wooden as coach). All the reporters would go to the iconic Pike Place Market to smell the fresh salmon and coho and chinooks. At CenturyLink Field, where the Seahawks play, the choices are mind-boggling: three locally made sausages with five different sauces; Pioneer Square's Rain Shadow Meats, served in a carton and dressed with capers, aioli, and arugula; or Kau Kau BBQ, roasted pork in a rice bowl. The chef himself spends the whole game walking the stadium to make sure everything's all right. I'm surprised Russell Wilson can stay on the field!

In New York, it's impossible, when going to a Knicks game or a college basketball game, to pick a restaurant among the thousands. If you' re in a hurry, go to a deli. If you can pick only one, go to Katz's Delicatessen on East Houston Street on the Lower East Side—it might have been there since the 1600s. Get the perfect slow-cured pastrami piled high. Like everyone, you will take a paper ticket when you walk in, and be prepared to order quickly when you get to the counter.

Because I met my husband, Bob, through Rick Pitino at the Derby, and had the privilege of covering the Triple

5:00 AM at the Kentucky Derby back stretch in 2004

Crown for ABC for almost a decade, Churchill Downs and Louisville will always be special to me. Everything in Louisville (named for King Louis XVI of France) comes with bourbon, but the best sandwich is the most iconic. Head to the Brown Hotel and order the Hot Brown, the famous turkey and bacon open-faced sandwich covered in Mornay sauce. If you have any room for breakfast during Derby Week, go to Wagner's Pharmacy, founded in 1922, located just outside Churchill Downs. You can sit beside trainers and track workers—legendary trainer Nick Zito first took me there in 1990. You can get sausages and biscuits and pick up some race tips by seven in the morning. But you can skip the mint julep, unless you like muddled mint and syrup. And it won't help you pick the winner.

CHAPTER 13

Thank God I loved and was loved by legendary *Globe* writer Will McDonough. If not, I would have been terrified of him. Half the NFL was in fear of him and so was the press corps. Will would be yelling on the phone at Al Davis in one ear and at Pete Rozelle in the other—and, of course, Coach Al and Commissioner Pete hated each other. All the sportswriters at the *Globe* would watch variations of this scene day after day with a mixture of pride and disbelief. And the people Will was fighting with loved him. In January of 2003, I was doing a story on the Oakland Raiders the morning Will died. Al Davis found me. We went to his office and cried. If I were in Baltimore or Miami, I used to go around practice saying, "Hi, I'm Lesley Visser, I work with Will McDonough." One time Don Shula, the most frightening block of granite himself, squinted his eyes and said, "You're friends with Will? That's great, let's have dinner." I almost fainted.

Another time, in about 1975, Will set up lunch for me at Art Rooney's house! Right there, in his old Victorian home in Pittsburgh across the street from where he'd grown up as the son of a saloon keeper. I couldn't even swallow the sandwich his beloved wife Kathleen brought to us in the living room. But Mr. Rooney made it easy, telling me about why he loved football and horse racing and how he'd tried to become an Olympic boxer. Everyone knew and adored "the Chief." By 1936, he'd become a sports legend when he parlayed a $500 bet at Saratoga into $300,000 over two days. He was a dominant yet calm person, and he seemed to genuinely enjoy the company of young people. It took Mr. Rooney from 1933 to 1975 to win a Super Bowl, but then the legendary Steelers were off to the races, winning three more champion- ships before most people finished breakfast. If you're ever at Heinz Field, there' s a wonderful statue of the Chief with "Gate D"—the only remaining piece of Three Rivers Stadium—standing high above his left shoulder. All the Rooneys were close to Will McDonough, and because of McDonough, the players and coaches were respectful. Yes, they thought I was young, but Will had told them that I would work hard, and he taught me to show up no matter what I had written.

I was always supported by McDonough, who taught me to laugh now and cry later. There was the time, in my first or second year on the Patriots beat, when the offensive line was banged up. Sam Cunningham was the running back then, the *older* brother of Randall, and Steve Grogan was the quarterback. Because of the injuries, I asked Coach Chuck Fairbanks who would start at right tackle, Tom Neville or Bob McKay. Fairbanks said, simply, "Either one can play the position." I went racing back to the *Globe*, thinking I had the scoop of a lifetime. The next morning, the headline read, "Coach Says 'Neither One Can Play the Position'"! My phone rang at 6:15 AM, and I heard Fairbanks screaming, "Are you out

With Dan Rooney and former *Globe* great Will McDonough at Heinz Field in 2002

of your mind? Why would I say no one can defend our quarterback or open up a running lane against the Miami Dolphins?" Click. As Will had taught me (and I can feel the chills today), I went down to the Patriots practice and took it like a man (more like a cowardly lion). Vince Doria reminds me of it to this day.

The Patriots were an interesting assortment, with a sloppy and funny history. But by 1976, the team was winning and even had the great John Hannah at left guard. Jess Phillips came to the team that year. He was smart and engaging. Born in Beaumont, Texas, he'd gone to Michigan State as a defensive back and played in one of the greatest college football games of all time, the

10–10 tie with undefeated Notre Dame. He majored in math and was drafted by the Bengals in 1968. Phillips bounced around a little, even switching to fullback, and came to the Patriots as a running back and kick returner.

His two years with the Patriots were relatively quiet. He was quick and funny, knew all about commodities and mortgage rates. He even spent a summer at the London School of Economics. He told me once he didn't understand why people would watch TV when they could be learning something new from a magazine. He was classy. I remember one night he ordered a single Chivas Regal and nursed it until closing time. He'd had one careless moment in college that cost him eight months in prison, which Will McDonough had told me about, but Phillips had grown up on a tree-lined street in a middle-class neighborhood. His father taught him to play football in the backyard.

It made Phillips's behavior in 1982 all the more bizarre. Five years out of the league, he held up a jewelry store in Reno, Nevada. On a rainy afternoon in April, Phillips went into Jay's Jewelers and asked to see all the gold bezels the small store had for sale. Jay's Jewelers had never had a holdup in twenty years. The workers were preparing to close around four thirty in the afternoon, when suddenly Phillips drew a gun from his briefcase and told everyone to hit the floor. Phillips tied their hands with surgical tape and was about to clean out the drawers when suddenly the front door bell rang. It was another customer.

Phillips ripped a cord from the adding machine, wrapped it around the customer, and pushed him to the floor. He then stuffed six diamonds and $400 in his pants and ran out the door. People outside saw the commotion and called the police. Considered kidnapping and robbery with a deadly weapon, the police immediately cleared all radio channels with the alert "Armed robbery in progress—Priority 1." The police said he ran like a deer. It even took five of them to stop the thirty-five-year-old former running back who knew how to throw a block. One officer tried to keep up with him on a motorcycle as Phillips flew down West Street.

They called out for him to stop, but he went into overdrive. Finally a bullet hit Phillips in the right arm and he collapsed in a basement stairwell. He'd been stupid and the perpetrator of a serious crime, and he'd done it with a pellet gun, which—unfortunately for him—met the standard for a deadly weapon in Nevada.

I went out to see Jess in prison. A lot of women, thankfully, never see the inside of a prison. It is a terrible place, with no carpet to absorb any sound, no fresh air, and no atmosphere of optimism. Back in 1982, Jess Phillips told me he didn't want me to see him like this, his arm bandaged, his spirit broken. He knew he'd done a terrible and senseless thing. Now in his late sixties, Phillips has turned his life around, writing a book about the history of stock futures and following the presidential debates. The experience of knowing him, of knowing people like Will McDonough and Art Rooney and Al Davis and Pete Rozelle, gave me such a deep perspective. Both the good and the bad. As Ellen DeGeneres says, "Life has to have a balance. The piña and the colada."

CHAPTER 14

I always tell people that sports is the ultimate passport—it takes you to places like Nagano, Japan, and Flowery Branch, Georgia. It takes you to housing projects in Chicago and majestic palaces in France. There are many lessons to be learned just from the travel alone. Add to that being around people who are the best at what they do and, voila! What a fantastic stew.

Being a woman—the first woman on most big events, both in print and in television—came with staggering opportunity and deep insecurity. I probably showed too much enthusiasm at first, but I wanted people to know that I would persevere, that a woman could be as good as everyone else. I mixed hard work (many nights in the *Boston Globe* library) with tennis games or pickup basketball during the day, acting like some kind of class secretary.

I've found that dressing the part doesn't hurt. I try not to go on planes in shorts and flip-flops; I try to be clean and proper for every interview. This doesn't mean staid, just appropriate. I think it makes people feel secure. When I go on vacation, it's another story. I wear sneakers everywhere, from the Trevi Fountain to the Grand Canyon. (By the way, did you know that tourists toss an average of

$22,000 into the Trevi Fountain every week? It goes to a charity that feeds the poor of Rome.)

I think young women still run harder to stay in place. But the rewards have been enormous. In 1986, I went back to Prague with Martina Navratilova, who hadn't returned to Communist Czechoslovakia since she'd defected ten years before. She won five *straight* Wimbledon titles (1982–86) and not one word had been written about her in the Czech media. She was considered a nonperson. In 1986, Martina went back to Prague as a member of the U.S. Federation Cup, the women's equivalent of the Davis Cup. Officially, no one said she was coming; it spread by word of mouth that the great Martina was coming home. And when she took the court, people cheered and cried. We all did.

One of my early events for CBS was a near disaster. It was at the U.S. Open in 1985, when another player from Prague, Hana Mandlíková, had a big win on an outer court. She was having a huge summer, going from something like fifty-fifth in the world up to fifth. After one of her early-round victories, our host, Brent Musberger, said, "Let's go to Lesley Visser, who's with Hana Mandlíková." Nervous and wooden, I said, "Hana, how do you account for your sudden rise in the rankings?"

And she said, in her thick Czech accent, "Vell, I sink it is my new couch."

Somewhat stunned, thinking maybe she was sleeping better, I stammered, "Oh, did you get some new furniture?"

She looked at me as if I were from Pluto and responded, "Don't be ridiculous, Betty Stove, my new coach."

Oops.

Interviewing all-time great tennis player Venus Williams in New York in 2009

All the years I covered tennis, from Bjorn Borg to Connors to McEnroe to Martina and Chris and Steffi Graf and Agassi and Sampras, I remember the thrill of being there for Serena Williams's eighteenth grand slam title at the U.S. Open against Caroline Wozniacki. Williams had the burden of trying to tie Evert and Navratilova in grand slam victories, and Wozniacki was both stunning and popular. I'll always remember when Serena joined the two great players, Evert and Navratilova, hugging the trophy as if it were her child.

There's almost no place I haven't been because of sports. I took a swim in the winter in Helsinki—which feels exactly

At the 2015 Final Four in Indianapolis

like it sounds—followed by a delicious sauna, and I got to see the Northern Lights from the airplane cockpit on my way to Edmonton, Canada, to cover the World Skating Championship, back in the mid-nineties when life was a lot looser. It was jaw-dropping, mystical, the way it spread out against the Canadian sky. Then we landed and I went to a production meeting. Sigh. Since half my life is flying to an event, I've become an expert on airports, and the two best—should you be headed that way—are Dubai and Singapore. Both have wonderful duty-free shops, great restaurants, and giant playgrounds for kids. Throw in a massage and you might not even need to see the city!

In 2001, I went to Shanghai for HBO's *Real Sports* to do the first American interview with a young Yao Ming. China was just emerging from Communism and it was thrilling. A wonderful producer, Valerie Gordon, and I spent a week with Yao and his family. Although we had a government "minder" and an interpreter the whole time, Yao took us to the famed promenade called the Bund and to the newer buildings that make up Shanghai's futuristic skyline. Yao only spoke English to me one time the entire week, but it was hilarious. When you do interviews in Communist countries, you ask the interpreter the question, then it goes through the government minder to the athlete, and the answer eventually loops back to the reporter. I asked the interpreter to elicit Yao's reaction to the fact that he earned $20,000 playing for the Chinese national team but he was about to make millions of dollars in the NBA. Before I could even finish the question, Yao cut me off, ignored the interpreter, and said, "I'll get used to it." Slam dunk.

The *Globe* would also send me to Marblehead, Massachusetts, considered the "sailing capital of the world," to cover the races along with expert John Ahern. The yacht clubs are gorgeous there; all of them look like Claude Monet's painting *The Garden at Sainte-Adresse*, with their wind-whipped flags flying free. John Ahern knew everybody—one time I heard him greet King Constantine of Greece in his Boston accent, "Connie, how the hell agh ya?"

There have been other events that I've witnessed, both good and bad for my soul. I was there in 1978 when Bucky F-ing Dent homered to beat the Red Sox after the Yankees had trailed by fourteen games in July. Living in New York all those years was like being in enemy territory. In the 2000 World Series, the Mets against the Yankees, I felt both electric and dismayed. In Game 1, when Roger Clemens threw the bat at Mike Piazza, everyone at Yankee Stadium was completely confused. I was there with my friend Carl Pascarella, the former CEO of Visa, and we didn't know what to think. My husband and I have become good friends with Piazza—we were his guests at his Hall of Fame induction in 2016—and now we have a better handle on what happened that day. Piazza, the greatest-hitting catcher of all time, doesn't talk much about the series, since he made the final out in Game 5 at Shea Stadium, but New York was riveted.

One beautiful series I got to work on was the Triple Crown for ABC, which meant we had Jim McKay hosting, Al Michaels and jockey Jerry Bailey in the booth, and the great Dave Johnson calling the horses as they were coming down the stretch. McKay once said the most

With ABC's Al Michaels at the Preakness Stakes in 1992

beautiful moment in sports is "the brown of the earth, the blue of the sky, the horses coming on to the track, and the University of Louisville band playing, 'My Old Kentucky Home.'" It was once called "the sport of kings" and it's easy to see why. It began in England when King Charles II and his pals started little racing meets. By 1762, the dukes and lords had their own racing silks. Now, in the state of Kentucky, the horse is king. I went to my first Derby in 1977, and I was blessed that *New York Times* writer Red Smith asked me to walk the infield. He would do this with a young writer every year, and it was an honor. Passing through the youthful enthusiasm of the infield is a lifetime experience, and Smith gave me some great advice: "Lesley, wherever

With the legendary Michael Jordan in the locker room before the 1997 NBA Finals. He told me to "stay sweet."

With Muhammad Ali at the 1992 Kentucky Derby

you are, whatever you are covering, look around—make a memory." I never forget those words, whether I'm in Istanbul or Knoxville, Tennessee.

I've always said that in my forty years of covering sports, there have been three people who could shift the dynamic of the room—people you knew were there even before you saw them: Muhammad Ali, Dan Marino, and Michael Jordan. Ali, who we lost in 2016, was the most significant, the ultimate athlete/activist. Millions of people were affected by the world champion, because he shook up our preconceived notions about boxers and poetry and blended it with jaw-dropping skill. Some people reading this, especially those younger than thirty-five, can't imagine Ali's force or radiance. His longtime corner man, Dr. Ferdie Pacheco, said he had an "inner excellence." I remember listening on a cheap radio on the night of March 8, 1971, when Ali fought Joe Frazier at Madison Square Garden and the fight went fifteen rounds. I was riveted, even though the updates only came every twenty minutes. Ali fought for what he believed in and he never backed down.

By contrast, I got fooled on O. J. Simpson. When I covered him as a player or worked with him in television, I thought he was the most charming, considerate person on the planet. And then, like everyone, I watched *People of the State of California v. Orenthal James Simpson* every day, compulsively, and came away with what many people believed: that the not-guilty verdict was based on lack of technical evidence. I'd only seen the playful side of O. J.; I knew nothing of his darkness. But I was in the

Kansas City Chiefs' locker room when the verdict came down on October 3, 1995. The verdict had been decided the day before, in only *four* hours, but Judge Ito decided to postpone the announcement until the following day. In Kansas City, players were milling around the locker room, and a small group of us from CBS were setting up for interviews. It was close to noon and suddenly everyone in the room stopped moving. The verdict was announced on TV, and I will never forget the scene. Every black player in the room cheered wildly and every white player looked shocked. The dueling themes—was he a sociopath or a nice guy who'd been framed?—were never fully answered. But the story of that moment in the Chiefs' locker room was simple: Our race relations were in terrible shape.

It was a tough observation for me, especially since most of the people I cover are African American and many of them are friends. We now have black coaches, black bosses, even a black president, but where are the boundaries and what can we learn? On the good side, sports is a cultural jambalaya, with people from all walks of life. Just think of your favorite team and what a mixture it is. Think of the three winning franchises coached by Pat Riley, the son of a cop from Schenectady, New York. He had Showtime with the Lakers, a physical Patrick Ewing and Charles Oakley team with the Knicks, and a beautifully balanced group in Miami.

Riley once told me that "defense is more about attitude than physical talent" and that the book he constantly read was *The Art of War* by Sun Tzu. I've since learned that many coaches turn to that book, because it teaches

With Los Angeles Lakers, New York Knicks, and Miami Heat basketball coach Pat Riley, who has nine championship rings

you to take a stand, no matter how tired you are. I love that about sports. People watching a game sometimes confuse the salary with the effort. Athletes carve out a vision on Day One—usually it's a championship—and how many of us can say that?

The great writer Dan Jenkins used to say, "Recognize the defining moments of your life and kick the hell out of them." This is the guy who gave us *Semi-Tough* and *Dead Solid Perfect*. Jenkins is the writer, along with the late Nora Ephron, that I wish I could be, funny and original and smart. I had a wonderful moment with Jenkins, although it didn't seem so at first. In a press box in the mid-seventies, I told him, "Dan you're what we all want to be." He looked at me and said, "What, hung over?"

In one of his books, *You Gotta Play Hurt*, he used me as a character. Her name was Jeannie, a young, ambitious sportswriter, while Tom was the older legend. The book takes place at sporting events from the Tour de France to the Indy 500 to the Masters—the ultimate passport. At one point, Jeannie and Tom go for a drink at Wimbledon at the famous pub called the Grenadier, on the corner of Wilton Row and Old Barrack Yard. Jack the Ripper drank there (of course, every London pub has a plaque that says the same thing), and Tom asks Jeannie about going to television. She says that CBS wants her. Angry to hear that, Tom says, "Why do you want to throw your writing away and spend the rest of your career saying, 'Back to you, Jim Nantz!'" Which, of course, is exactly what I've done since I left the *Boston Globe*.

And I've loved every minute. I did one of the last interviews with the legendary Pat Summitt, and it was painful because she couldn't remember any of her eight national championships with Tennessee. But producer Charlie Bloom handled her Alzheimer's beautifully, never embarrassing the iconic coach. Once I went bowling with Pittsburgh Steeler Jerome Bettis, who brought his own shoes and bowling ball. He beat me by 100 points. I also went horseback riding with Emmitt Smith and golfing with Marshall Faulk, both well beyond my abilities. My favorite player to watch was Lawrence Taylor, the Hall of Fame New York Giants linebacker, who was always testing positive for something. One time, on camera, I asked him what his problem was. He kind of laughed, looked down at the floor, and said, "I'll tell you what the problem is—my drug dealer lives five minutes away and takes American Express."

After forty years of being around greats, near-greats, bust-ups, addicts, and billionaires, I hope I've learned some lessons about both humor and value. I read a book by *New York Times* columnist David Brooks and he put it into perspective. He said we all have two résumés. We have our work résumé, hopefully filled with bright stars and career success. And we have our moral résumé, virtues filled with goodness and light and things people talk about at funerals: Were you kind, were you brave, did you stand up for others? I had the privilege of being one of five speakers at the memorial service for Bud Collins—I spoke after Chris Evert and before Billie Jean King—and everyone had the same message about his moral résumé. That Bud was simply the nicest person we'd ever met, that he'd had a brilliant career and an even deeper inner light. At his request, his wife Anita spread his ashes at Wimbledon, and the only epitaph I ever heard that came close to what he asked her to do was when the great coach Bear Bryant was asked what he wanted his headstone to read. He answered quickly, "Never could beat Notre Dame."

BEARS
2005
GAME ONE
CBS
10819
CBS SPORTS
PACKERS
PRESS BOX
DIVISIO
NFL
LESLEY VISSER
CBS SPORTS
VS.
SUNDAY
PRESS BOX
GAME
6
0059
LAMBEAU FIELD
1957-2007
AUTHORIZED BY
DATE
AFFILIATION
NAME
Lesley Visser
CBS
Sept 7 2008
CBS SPORTS

CHAPTER 15

The greatest scene in movie history is at the end of *Some Like It Hot* when Joe E. Brown finds out that Jack Lemmon isn't the woman he's been dressed up to be. Brown looks at him and says, "Well, nobody's perfect." Certainly not me or anybody I knew, except maybe Bud Collins or Dick Enberg or James Brown. But I made plenty of mistakes. I had people be loyal to me when it counted and people betray me when it hurt.

My toughest defeat came in front of the whole country. I had been named the first woman in the history of *Monday Night Football*, and I loved working with Al Michaels, Dan Dierdorf, Boomer Esiason, and Frank Gifford. For reasons unknown to me, Kenny Wolfe, our *Monday Night Football* producer, who'd played basketball at Harvard, didn't get along with new management at ABC, even though he'd been on *MNF* for a dozen years. I got a call in the middle of the summer from John Filippelli, a good man who later ran the YES Network for the Yankees. He told me *that day* that ABC was announcing I'd be let go. Out went Wolfe, Esiason, and myself, and in came Don Ohlmeyer as producer. He replaced me with twenty-six-year old Melissa Stark—I think she was as shocked as I was.

When I was replaced, l was devastated. It was even on the front page of *USA Today*, above the *Kuwaiti oil prices*! My then-husband Dick Stockton bought as many papers as he could and hid them in the piano bench. ABC said I could work on the evening news or a Sunday show, but I was stunned. The NFL sent me a crystal football thanking me for being the first woman on *MNF* and doing such a good job, and someone sent me a note quoting a line by poet Emily Dickinson: "Fear not, the brain is wider than the sky."

I had covered the NFL for three decades; I knew the players and the game, and ABC's *Monday Night Football* was the number-one show on television. I was having a blast. I got along great with the producers and stayed out of the way of the booth, where associate producer Steve Hirdt kept Al Michaels sane before kickoff. I remember one game we did in Green Bay that was Al's favorite moment in all the times we worked together. Al despised the Clinton administration and was always talking about it. On this night at Lambeau Field, I did a sideline interview with former quarterback Bart Starr. It was during the time that President Clinton was being investigated, and l ended the interview by saying, "There you have it, Al, the Starr report."

Al howled. He mentioned it for weeks.

Dan Dierdorf was another kind of fun, and I think he was the only player who walked to his Hall of Fame Induction. Raised in Canton, Ohio, Dan had size and speed and quickness and intelligence. His University of Michigan education also gave him a great vocabulary. During dinners, he would talk about playing for Bo

Schembechler in college and Don Coryell in the pros. One time when we were in St. Louis, he took me to lunch with his old pal and former teammate Conrad Dobler, once labeled the "dirtiest player in the league." I was terrified, but Dobler was proud and said he played fair, which was kind of curious since he was known for leg-whipping or even biting opponents. Dierdorf would just shake his head and laugh. No one was a better host than Dan Dierdorf and no one had a better laugh.

After the call from Filippelli, I went into a shell for ten hours, curled up and reread a line from Hemingway's *A Farewell to Arms*: "The world breaks everyone and afterward many are strong at the broken places." Two of my friends came over in the morning to take me away. Kelly Neal (now Naqi) and Heather Albert (wife of Marv) said, "We're leaving for Paris." I couldn't get on their flight, so I left on the next flight, and CBS CEO Les Moonves just happened to be on the same flight. He said only one thing to me as he moved easily into his seat. "You're not staying at ABC, you're coming back to CBS."

And I did. And I've been happy about it ever since, which is now more than fifteen years. They've stayed with me and I've stayed with them, even during some dicey times. One weekend, after I'd shattered my hip and was laid up in bed for months, I learned all the words to "Brown Sugar," Greg Gumbel's favorite song. He's close friends with the Rolling Stones (they once consulted *him* about their set list for a tour—can you imagine?), so I wanted to get the words right. When I came back to the *NFL Today* set, Greg welcomed me. I told him I'd learned his song and started to sing it. He shut me off, saying we

With the incomparable CBS CEO Les Moonves

While visiting Les Moonves at home in Malibu, 1994

had to go to commercial, just as I was deep into "ship bound for cotton fields . . ." Greg turned to the camera and said, "The thanks of a grateful nation." Humph.

After I was let go, *Monday Night Football* bounced around and went to ESPN; Al Michaels left for NBC, and John Madden went with him. Ohlmeyer lasted exactly one year as *MNF* producer; he had to hire a sideline producer to stand with Stark during games, and she was gone two years after that. Now *Sunday Night Football* on NBC is the place to be, where Al Michaels, Chris Collinsworth, and Michele Tafoya have settled into a gold-standard group.

I had other embarrassing moments. I tried everything I could think of to keep my feet warm in places like Soldier Field, Giants Stadium, or Foxborough. One time in Green Bay, I bought battery-operated socks—with big batteries that hung out the back of my boots and went dead in the second quarter as I was galumphing around the field. On the air, John Madden said it was the most pathetic thing he'd ever seen. Another time, CBS thought it would be great if I took batting practice at the World Series. You can imagine how that went. I never came close to connecting and had nine innings to get over my humiliation.

The darkest hour in sports, of course, was the massacre in Munich in 1972, when Palestinian terrorists invaded the Israeli dormitory at the Olympic Village and the ensuing bloodbath cost seventeen lives and inflicted deep psychological terror. My mini-dark hour was in 1986, when the Red Sox had thirteen third-strike pitches to win the World Series over the Mets. My assignment was the Red Sox clubhouse celebration—whee, after

At the 2004 Houston Super Bowl pregame party with Jim Nantz, CBS
Sports Chairman Sean McManus, Greg Gumbel, and Hall of Fame
running back Marcus Allen

With CBS announcer Greg Gumbel at the 2012 Final Four

sixty-eight years! With the Sox leading and two outs in the bottom of the tenth, Shea Stadium's scoreboard flashed, "Congratulations to the Boston Red Sox, 1986 World Champions." Of course, it was not to be. And it unraveled so quickly, when Bill Buckner let Mookie Wilson's baby ground ball bobble between his legs. Ray Knight skipped home with the winning run and I ended up doing a story on Kevin Mitchell. The Sox, of course, lost in Game 7 and Buckner moved to Idaho. Next?

On one or two occasions, the embarrassment ended up being on the other person. For some reason, I got over being afraid of Bobby Knight, the brilliant coach from Indiana. One time in the NCAA Tournament, the Hoosiers beat Temple in the Regional Semifinal. I asked Knight about it after the game and he said, "Well, you may not have noticed, but we scored more points—you people in the media sometimes miss that." I laughed and said, "Yeah, yeah, yeah, how did you handle their matchup zone?" Then Knight started laughing and we've been friends ever since. I got a standing ovation in the press room. Like the ad says, sometimes the greatest risk is not taking one. I loved the coaches who didn't cheat—Knight, Krzyzewski, Izzo, Carril—and I had admiration for all of them. It's extremely hard to recruit and teach and strive to make the NCAA tournament. Many coaches have cut corners to get it done.

I had another embarrassing moment (do you think I'm a loser?) at one of the tournaments in the early 1980s. The coaches always had their own hotel, and I had a standing date with the brilliant writers John Feinstein of the *Washington Post* and Dick Weiss of the *Philadelphia*

Daily News to go over to the lobby and say hello to our friends. This was when Roy Williams and Bill Self were kids in the business, just like we were. I remember going up to the great Pete Newell, the California and Olympic coach, and saying, "I just want to thank you for all you've done for college basketball, what a giant you've been." He looked at me with a screwed-up face, thanked me, and walked away. I went back to Feinstein and Weiss and told them of my epiphany and they said, "Well, that's nice, but that's not Pete Newell, that's Charlie Spoonhour of Southwest Missouri State."

Wanna get away?

But I soldiered on. I went to practices, games, and press conferences, and one time tried to run Feinstein over. Feinstein, Weiss, and I spent our lives together, all covering the same events at the same time, all over the country. One year in Ann Arbor, Michigan, Feinstein had really irritated me and I tried to run him over with my rent-a-car in the parking lot. He stuck out his Portabubble (these big computers we had back then) to defend himself and he somehow managed to live. I couldn't sleep after this horrific event, and he was and is one of my best friends, so that night, in our crummy motel, I called his room. The phone rang a few times, he picked up, and I started in, "John, I'm so sorry, I love you . . ." And all I heard was, "Zzzzzzzz, zzzzzzz" really loud. I hung up, stunned and furious. Can I chalk this up to boys, or is that sexist?

I have learned many things while covering sports and I would give this advice above all others, from a song by Lee Ann Womack. I'm sure many of you remember it, but

Interviewing Atlanta Falcons quarterback Matt Ryan at the NFC
Championship Game versus San Francisco in 2013

sing it to yourself: "And when you get the choice to sit it out or dance, I hope you dance!"

I've had many, many more embarrassing moments in my forty years, but I'll leave this chapter with Mary Decker. You might not remember, but she was the great American middle-distance runner who was heavily favored in the 1984 Olympics in Los Angeles. She had won gold medals at the World Track Championships in both the 1,500- and 3,000-meter events and she was training twice a day in Eugene, Oregon, in preparation for the Games. In 1983, CBS sent me to do a story with her. We agreed to meet in the hotel lobby and take, in her words, "a light jog while we do the interview." I was no runner, but I was no slouch, running five miles a day . . . only Mary ran ten miles a day at six minutes a mile. We left the hotel and I asked her how she was preparing for the Games in L.A., where her rival, Zola Budd, would be her undoing when she tripped Mary and ruined her opportunity for Olympic gold. Mary said she was running twice a day, stretching, and doing push-ups because "You need upper body strength in the final yards." That was the answer to my first question. By the second question, she had sprinted so far beyond me that I had to yell, "OH, MARY!" That was the end of the interview.

CHAPTER 16

Everyone always asks me my favorite event in sports, and I always say it's the semifinals of the Final Four. On that Saturday, every school thinks it has a chance and all four of them do. You might say, "No way," that one team is clearly the best, but I've been there when NC State beat Houston, when Villanova beat Georgetown, and when Butler almost won the title. Jim Calhoun built a dynasty out of the desert and won three titles for Connecticut. Pitino took Providence to the Final Four. It isn't always powerhouses, like when North Carolina beat Michigan State at sold out Ford Field in 2009, but sometimes those are great games, too.

The best basketball game I was ever a part of or witness to happened in 1992, when Grant Hill found Christian Laettner to beat Kentucky in the Regional Finals in Philadelphia. Verne Lundquist, Lenny Elmore, and I were on the broadcast, and we all heard Mike Krzyzewski say in the huddle, "Grant, can you throw it?" and, "Christian, can you catch it?" Not, "Can you make a perfect pass?" or "Can you make the shot?" Grant Hill said people had forgotten that he played high school football. Pitino decided not to guard the inbounds pass, and Hill threw it perfectly. Laettner calmly put the ball on the floor, pivoted, and

made the shot at the buzzer. He was ten for ten from the
field and ten for ten from the line. The spectacular finish
gave Duke the historic 104–103 win. I had to wait for the
postgame interview because as soon as the game ended,
Krzyzewski walked down press row to shake hands with
legendary Kentucky announcer Cawood Ledford, who
was retiring after thirty-nine years.

There have been so many moments, in every sport,
that are both personally and professionally meaningful,
but my biggest assignment was not a sporting event.
It was the fall of the Berlin Wall. On the evening of
November 9, 1989, East Germany announced the "easing
of travel restrictions" to West Berlin—a simple statement
that changed the world. CBS Sports, in a brave decision

Covering the fall of the Berlin Wall for CBS in 1989

by executive producer Ted Shaker, sent me to do a story on how sports would change in East Germany once the wall came down. The GDR (German Democratic Republic, its official name) had been insignificant economically, but a giant athletically. From 1976 until 1988, the GDR finished second in both the Summer and Winter Olympics, and at the 1980 Games in Moscow (which the United States boycotted), the GDR won forty-seven gold, thirty-seven silver, and forty-two bronze medals, second only to the USSR. With a population of only sixteen million, the country was staggeringly successful in athletics and widely believed to be doping at every level of its twenty-five state-sponsored sport schools.

I went to Berlin with producer Ed Goren, later a big cheese at Fox, and producer/interpreter Draggan Mihailovich, who become one of the main producers at *60 Minutes*. We had visas and interviews set up, and in the meantime, we chipped away at the Wall and saved the souvenirs in small plastic bags. None of us could believe we were witnessing the story of the century. For nearly three decades, the Berlin Wall had been a symbol of repression, an eleven-foot-high concrete barrier topped by barbed wire that prevented the people of East Berlin from being free. The inner German border was officially closed in 1952, but people still left through Hungry to get to freedom in Austria. The Berlin Wall was not erected until 1961. Construction began under the advice and counsel of Nikita Khrushchev, who, like the socialist chairman of the GDR, Walter Ulbricht, was worried about the "brain drain"—the emigration of engineers, doctors, lawyers, and smart young people to West Berlin, Austria, or beyond. Khrushchev and Ulbricht felt the exodus had to be stopped, even though our young president, John F. Kennedy, had declared himself a Berliner in June 1963. The world was watching, but East Germany didn't care.

The Wall wasn't just a short divide between East and West Berlin. It was eighty-seven miles long, with a 100-yard field between two fences known as the "death strip." The strip was covered with sand so that footprints could easily be seen by the East German border guards, who were ordered to shoot on sight. Reinforced concrete barricades were added to further deter would-be defectors—a bed of nails was even added near the top of the Wall. There were 116 watchtowers, multiple lines of trained dogs, and at least twenty bunkers. The people of East Germany weren't going anywhere. If you're ever in Washington, DC, it's worth a trip to the Newseum, which has four original panels of the Berlin Wall, plus a guard tower. You'll feel exactly how chilling an attempted escape had been back then. There were nine official crossings, the most famous, of course, being Checkpoint Charlie, which was restricted to Allied personnel and foreigners.

We had a visa to cross at Checkpoint Charlie, officially the corner of Friedrichstrasse and Zimmerstrasse, to do an interview with Katarina Witt, the figure skater from Karl-Marx-Stadt, East Germany (now called Chemnitz). *Time* had called her "The Most Beautiful Face of Socialism," and she was paraded around as the symbol of success in the GDR. In East Berlin, we sat on some bleachers in an old skating rink, and I remember her being charming and guarded. She'd been raised, after all, in the strict disciplines of skating and Communism. She would not talk about any doping scandal or the separation of families because of the Wall, or even her world *behind* the Wall. And there was no way she was going to address the topic of the Stasi—the East German secret police, which employed 90,000 people to spy on ordinary citizens. The Stasi definitely had a file on her. They'd even chronicled her first sexual encounter in their secret archives, which were opened in 1992.

Witt was different as a young athlete. She was once called so pretty she would cause "a 12-car-pileup." She did, after all, pose for *Playboy* in December 1998. Witt said she did it because athletes from Soviet Bloc countries were seen as stiff and robotic, which many of them appeared to be. Now we know that many of them were terrified of the government and most likely doping. The East German government knew the popularity and power of Katarina Witt. Although everything was controlled, she had a nicer apartment, easier travel restrictions, and better food than many East Germans.

On the day we met her, she was happy to discuss her gold medal in Sarajevo and a second gold at the Games in Calgary. After Ronald Regan implored Soviet president Mikhail Gorbachev to "tear down this wall" in June 1987, the protests got louder and the world joined in. I had heard stories from my stepmother, Barbara, whose family had walked from Dresden to get through the Brandenburg Gate and taste freedom, with nothing on their backs. The Wall was finally dismantled in November of 1989, and Katarina Witt went on tour in the United States with the brilliant skater Brian Boitano. She now runs a production company in Berlin and endorses everything from BMWs to German cosmetics.

It was our only day in East Berlin, and I was struck by some of the grandiose Stalinist architecture. Most of the buildings were drab, as were the skies, but here and there you could see a slice of what it might have been. There was a stately boulevard, Karl-Marx-Allee, and a couple of parks, but the people shuffled along quickly, wearing watches with wristbands that said CCCP. The few cars on the streets, which were just pulled up in front of the dirty buildings, were Trabants—the most common car in East Germany, with an inefficient two-stroke engine that emitted a dangerously smoky exhaust. I remember one time I had to use a bathroom and we stopped at a hotel. The toilet paper was close to sandpaper, and I told the camera crew I wouldn't complain ever again.

We did a few more interviews to try and give the piece some perspective, but I think the stand-up I did in front of the Wall really summed it up. Goren told me to write something that would reflect how enormous the occasion was, and what we might see. I had covered Wimbledon that year, and it had been won by the flamboyant Boris Becker, who was born in West Germany. I mentioned him, the luck of the draw, and finished my stand-up by saying we could only wonder how many great athletes would now come from "the other side of the Wall." Most of the great athletes who were born in what used to be East Germany, though, have now moved to the West for better training and better opportunities. The next doping scandal moved to Russia.

CHAPTER 17

Minneapolis in the winter is beautiful: frozen lakes, clear skies, and the gorgeous Swedish Institute for hot chocolate, plus a glimpse of how the Scandinavians settled here with their ornate woodwork and complicated tile. When the Super Bowl was there in January 1992, John Madden suggested that we take his bus north and go ice fishing. Remember the line by singer Bob Seger, "Wish I didn't know now what I didn't know then"? That song was written for ice fishing. What a terrible sport— freezing, wet, cutting wind, hardly any fish. Mille Lacs, Minnesota, the huge freshwater lake one hundred miles north of Minneapolis up Highway 169, is enormously popular in the winter, and the walleye fish are supposed to be plentiful. Ha! We hardly caught any. And a walleye is about the most unattractive thing you've ever seen. It looks at you from both sides of its head, like some kind of Marty Feldman, plus it's got a giant Carol Channing mouth and oily skin. Hard to believe it's the state fish of Minnesota (and also Vermont—what were they thinking?).

Mille Lacs ("One Thousand Lakes" in French) drains into the Mississippi River, but in the winter, it freezes four feet deep and is desolate, except for the ice fishing houses: sort of A-frame playhouses that sit in the middle of the lake, with rugs on the floor and toasty blankets for the shivering participants. Madden said we couldn't rent an ice house, that we would fish off of turned-over buckets, because "ice houses are for chickenshits." We stopped along the way north to get our gear: long underwear, wool socks, big mittens called "choppers," and heavy, thick boots. There were seven of us, and we had no idea what we were getting into. The Madden Cruiser went to the edge of the lake (forty-two feet deep), and we walked, like spacemen on the moon, to the middle with our short poles and plastic buckets. Our guide—hired on the spot—drilled ten-inch holes for us, where we dropped our lures, which were some disgusting combination of nightcrawlers and bugs.

We were told there would be no "goofing around or loud talk"—two of my favorite things—because there were serious fishermen on the lake who were not to be distracted. Walleye, we were told, bite best just before sundown, so we sat there for hours. Did I mention I was freezing? Did I mention that not talking for four hours froze my jaw shut? Mille Lacs was settled by the Ojibwe tribe (part of the Chippewa) in the 1700s. They endured by hunting deer and moose and small game—nothing about fishing for walleye. I kept saying to myself, "I'm only five hundred miles from Chicago, I bet I could walk there." But then something great happened. The sun went down and we took our ten crummy fish back to the Madden Cruiser. On the two-hour trip back to Minneapolis, producer Lance Barrow cleaned the fish and fried up a pan full of walleye filets, swimming in butter and sprinkled with basil and salt. The fresh fish was the best thing any of us had ever eaten!

Ice fishing with John Madden before Super Bowl XXVI, the game where I became the only woman to ever present the Lombardi Trophy. We drove his Madden Cruiser one hundred miles north to Mille Lacs and fished for walleye.

I went fishing one other time, with the late, great Denny Green, coach of Northwestern, Minnesota, and Arizona. I had known him since the eighties, when he was at Northwestern, and one time in Minneapolis he said we should go fishing. Denny had been a fisherman for four decades, loving to debate purple worms or Texas-style rigs. He once caught a six-pound smallmouth bass in Minnesota and an eight-pounder in Florida. I could have cared less, but he had gone 11–5 with the Vikings and lost the NFC Championship badly to the Giants. If we had to go fishing to talk about what happened, so be it.

We went to Lake Minnetonka, just west of Minneapolis (obviously my kind of fishing town). Denny wanted to go at 6 AM, but I said, "No way." He didn't like big fish hunting, just riding around on his little bass boat, enjoying the day. I had little interest in any of his fishing memories (trawling the Susquehanna River as a kid or the rock quarries in Iowa City), I just wanted to know about Randy Moss. But we were old friends so I tried to enjoy it. Denny was a real angler; he even had a one-day tournament in Minnesota for more than five years. I couldn't stand the sight of worms, green or purple. Or even old Purple People Eaters. But we spent three hours on the water and had a blast. I even caught a fish.

I've been involved with other animals. I bought two thoroughbreds with my buddy Rick Pitino. That was a disaster. They were beautifully bred at Claiborne Farm, where Secretariat stood, but these horses had psychological problems. When the gate would open before a race, one of them would just stand there, like he was the spectator. I told Rick we shouldn't feed him if he didn't want to work. The other horse just looked away whenever anyone approached. I don't know if he didn't like people or didn't like what they wanted him to do. One of them was named "Rock Oliver" after Rick's old strength coach. Every time I saw Rock, I tried to extort money from him. The other was called Monte D'oro, mountain of gold. More like mountain of dust. After changing trainers about every two months, and trying to win races from every small track in Kentucky to the mighty Saratoga, we finally sold the horses. I told Rick I could have had the same experience driving down the Jersey Turnpike, "throwing my money out the window."

With seven-time NCAA Basketball Final Four participant and Hall of Fame coach Rick Pitino

CHAPTER 18

After covering thirty-five Super Bowls, a few of them really stand out. One of them was Super Bowl XXXVI, in 2002, almost five months after 9/11. The entire city, country—every heart, every emotion—just shut down on that day. At the time I was living on the Upper East Side. A group of us, not knowing what to do, went over to a

With 940 AM host Jeff DeForrest on Radio Row at Super Bowl XLII in 2008. Photo by Paula Breck.

Reporting from a Minnesota Vikings playoff game in Minnesota in 2010

hospital on First Avenue and lined up to give blood. Thank God, the line was three hours long, because everyone else had the same idea.

My relationships were strong enough with both the Giants and the Jets that CBS sent me to Ground Zero with both teams to hand out sandwiches and water to the first responders—the firefighters, policemen, and first-aid workers. Many people don't remember that Joe Andruzzi, an offensive anchor for the Patriots for many years, had three brothers who were firefighters and all first responders at Ground Zero. Their father and mother, Bill and Mary Ann, living on Staten Island with all communication shut down, didn't hear from their sons for a

With brother Chris at the 2000 Super Bowl

week, not knowing if they were dead or alive somewhere in the seven stories of rubble. All of them lived, but one is still deeply shaken by what he saw more than fifteen years ago.

I went to thirteen funerals, and the country was so depressed that I will be forever grateful to the late Wellington Mara, who offered me a ride on the Giants' charter plane to Kansas City when the NFL resumed playing a week later. All the airports were still closed. At that game in Arrowhead Stadium, I will never forget when the Giants stood in the tunnel ready to take the field and all the Kansas City fans reached down to touch them as the players reached up to grab their hands. We were one country, indivisible. During the game, the late,

With former Red Sox manager and New York Yankees bench coach
Don Zimmer at an event honoring those who died on 9/11

great sportsman Lamar Hunt, owner of the Chiefs, passed
firemen's boots throughout the stadium to be filled with
dollars and sent back to New York.

I guess that's why my favorite Super Bowl was the
Patriots' first win in Super Bowl XXXVI in New Orleans,
when New England beat St. Louis, 20–17. The Rams were
heavily favored, with a 14–2 record and the nickname
"The Greatest Show on Turf." The game ended when Adam
Vinatieri kicked a 48-yarder as time ran out, only five
months after the terrorist attacks. At the end of the game,
my brother Chris and I were on the field (he said I practically broke his hand from squeezing it so hard) as the red,
white, and blue confetti rained down on the Superdome

field and Patriot owner Robert Kraft said simply, "Today, we are all Patriots."

For sheer entertainment, the Velcro catch on David Tyree's head as Rodney Harrison tried to pull him down, and the touchdown pass from Eli Manning to Plaxico Burress to spoil the Patriots' perfect season, rank as number two for me, with the Giants winning, 17–14, in Super Bowl XLII. The pregame drama was unequaled—finally, someone was going to challenge the Dolphins' undefeated season from 1972—but Tyree almost didn't play with an upset stomach. Yet he somehow caught the ball after Manning imitated Houdini to get free, followed by Burress's heart-pounding reception in the corner of

With my mentor and friend Robert Kraft, owner/CEO of the New England Patriots

the end zone. The whole sequence was unique for its sheer tension. Coach Tom Coughlin had to look up on the Jumbotron to see if Plaxico caught the ball because the team was past the sideline, standing and jumping in front of him. I don't think Glendale, Arizona, has been the same since.

My third favorite championship was personal. In Super Bowl XXXIV, Atlanta had been through an ice storm and driving was terrible, all slippery and slow. The morning of the game, tight end Roland Williams, who was always upbeat, told me that if I had a slice of "Grandmama's pecan pie" the Rams would win. I did and they did. The first half of the game was defensive (although Tina Turner sang "Proud Mary" to lift the spirits in the Georgia Dome at halftime). The Rams had a 23–16 lead in the fourth quarter, and on the last play of the game, I was on the Rams sideline, only two yards from the end zone. (I was with ABC; it was the first game broadcast in high-definition.) Steve McNair hit six-foot Kevin Dyson on a slant. As Dyson was moving toward the end zone to tie the game, Rams linebacker Mike Jones saw him out of the corner of his eye and lunged. As Dyson was tackled, he stretched out his arm, bowing his tendon, to try and cross the goal line, but Jones held tight and Dyson fell inches short. NFL Films made a movie of the final play called "The Longest Yard."

So many Super Bowls have meant so much to so many. I was privileged to be the first woman on the sideline of a Super Bowl, for ABC in Miami, when Steve Young threw six touchdown passes and the 49ers crushed San Diego; and I became the only woman to present the Lombardi

Trophy, in 1992 at Super Bowl XXVI, when Washington beat Buffalo 37–24, but those were personal highs. It was also the year I became the first woman sportscaster in a Super Bowl commercial. Remember when Michael Jordan and Larry Bird played H.O.R.S.E.? McDonald's had rented and painted old Joe Robbie Stadium for the filming, and this is how the script went. Two mooks showed up at the game and expected to get seats. When the ticket window shut them down, they sat down on a bench and ate a couple of Big Macs. Suddenly Michael Jordan said to them, "Hey, you guys need a couple of tickets? I'm kinda busy here." They practically choked and the music was orchestral. The next scene was Jordan and Bird deciding to play H.O.R.S.E. for a large wager. Larry's line was, "Through the goalposts, around the bench, off Lesley Visser's head." This was all fine, except Bird kept slurring, "off Lezi Vissah's head." Cut. I got to play myself on the sideline and even ad-libbed a line, but I was getting a migraine headache because we had to keep doing it every time Bird messed up.

When the advertising agency, Leo Burnett in Chicago, first called me and said, "Lesley, how would you like to do a Super Bowl commercial, with Michael Jordan and Larry Bird, for McDonald's?" I stammered and said, "Really . . . I'll pay YOU!" My agent was furious; he said it cost me about $100,000. After three hours of the basketball bouncing off my head, I wasn't sure whatever the salary was would be worth it, but the commercial came out great. To this day, it's voted one of the most popular Super Bowl commercials, and my family plays it every year.

A few years before that, I was shocked to be named the presenter of the winning Lombardi trophy at the Super Bowl. That honor had usually gone to people like Brent Musburger or Terry Bradshaw. But executive producer Ted Shaker decided that I could handle it, and it would be historic, the first woman to handle the trophy presentation. My strongest memory was asking a question of Redskins owner Jack Kent Cooke, who was not shy—after all, he owned the Los Angeles Forum and the Chrysler Building in New York. Cooke took the microphone from my hand and rambled on about his life selling *Encyclopaedia Britannica* door to door as a child in Canada, how he got into real estate and finally bought the Redskins— while this was being beamed to 130 countries around the world! Producer Bob Stenner was screaming in my ear, "Get the goddamn microphone out of Jack Kent Cooke's hand!" I was trying not to act nervous, and people like Commissioner Paul Tagliabue and Coach Joe Gibbs, both gentlemen, made it much easier on me. I think I might have had an extra margarita that night.

Historically great football championships have included Super Bowl III, when Broadway Joe "guaranteed" a win over Baltimore (although we can't forget Johnny Unitas wasn't at his best all year), or John Elway helicoptering his way toward the end zone in Super Bowl XXXII in 1998, or anytime Brett Favre took the field. The Steelers' Super Bowls were the stuff of memory, none better than Super Bowl X, when Terry Bradshaw's 64-yard touchdown pass to Lynn Swann and a near-perfect defense beat the Cowboys. Another great game was Super Bowl

XLIII, Pittsburgh's 27–23 win over Arizona in 2009. Just close your eyes and think of Santonio Holmes on tiptoes with the winning catch, or the epic 100-yard James Harrison interception. Super Bowl XXV had two New York teams, the war in Iraq, Whitney Houston's national anthem, and Scott Norwood's 47-yard field goal attempt that sailed right and will live eternally alongside Chris Webber calling time out at the Final Four and the Red Sox selling Babe Ruth. Everyone has a favorite Super Bowl, and some teams (like the 49ers or Steelers or Patriots) have a handful to choose from.

Here are two nuggets I learned during Super Bowl weeks that maybe you've heard and maybe you haven't. You know, of course, it wasn't even called the Super Bowl until the Jets beat the Colts in Miami—before that it was the AFL–NFL World Championship. But before you complain about your salary, the Packers got $15,000 each for winning and the Chiefs earned $7,500.

One of my strongest NFL memories, a game that really sums up everything I've known and loved about sports, was the 1996 NFC Championship in Green Bay. Before the game, the Packers played a video of Reggie White saying the words to "Amazing Grace." Even the Carolina Panther players were moved. Carolina led at halftime, and it took the greatness of Brett Favre, Dorsey Levens, and Reggie White to bring the Packers back to their first NFC title in twenty-nine years. After the game, the University of Wisconsin band played "Roll Out the Barrel" and Reggie, who died too young, ran around the field with the Halas Trophy held high as a light snow fell. I thought I was the luckiest girl in the world.

With the late, great defensive end from the Philadelphia Eagles and the Green Bay Packers, Reggie White

I used to have to interview the singer at every Super Bowl, which meant that one year my little white hand got lost in Diana Ross's huge hair as she belted out "God Bless America." She also insisted (it was in her contract) that she couldn't be seen on the field near the Oscar Meyer "Wienermobile." I am not making this up. Jim Steeg, a quiet, intelligent man who ran Super Bowl week for twenty-six years, everything from Radio Row to half-times, had to deal with things like this. Usually, the talent was Carol Channing (Who? Believe me, she was big.) or Up with People—a sort of "We Are the World" chorus group. One year in Pasadena, Disney produced "It's a Small World" for halftime. The whole scene didn't really

Interviewing Hall of Famer Brett Favre on the field after the NFC
playoff game

On-site at Super Bowl XXXVIII in Houston, Texas, with Jim Nantz, Dan Marino, Deion Sanders, and Boomer Esiason. Photo by John P. Filo/CBS ©2004 CBS Broadcasting Inc. All rights reserved.

take off until Jim McMahon mooned a helicopter when the Bears played in New Orleans in Super Bowl XX, and the next year, Phil Simms became the first quarterback to go to Disney World after the Giants beat the Broncos.

Super Bowl XXII in San Diego became famous when Washington quarterback Doug Williams thought a reporter had asked him, "How long have you been a black quarterback?" and the next year in Miami, Bengals running back Stanley Wilson talked about overcoming his drug addiction and then wasn't seen for days, which sort of ended his NFL career. Super Bowl halftimes started to take off when Michael Jackson performed at Super Bowl

With Chicago coach Lovie Smith and Indianapolis coach Tony Dungy
at a pregame Super Bowl LXI dinner in Miami. Photo by Jeffrey R.
Staab/CBS ©2007 CBS Broadcasting Inc. All Rights Reserved.

XXVII. U2 performed one year, as did Bruce Springsteen, Paul McCartney, and Madonna. For Super Bowl XXXV in Tampa, Baltimore coach Brian Billick asked Hank Aaron to address the team, and the Ravens promptly went out and beat the Giants. Of course, they also had Ray Lewis. Super Bowl XXXVIII in Houston featured the infamous Janet Jackson "wardrobe malfunction," where CBS's LeslieAnne Wade and Gil Schwartz had to go into public relations overdrive, and few people even remember how great the Patriots–Panthers fourth quarter was. At Super Bowl XL in Detroit, there was a five-second delay on the Rolling Stones performance, because it was feared the lyrics to their songs "Brown Sugar" and "Rough Justice" might be considered offensive.

Jerry Jones was embarrassed, for maybe the first time, when his new Cowboys Stadium in Arlington wasn't quite finished for Super Bowl XLV. More than twelve hundred seats weren't ready, and Christina Aguilera flubbed the National Anthem. But Packer fans were happy; they beat the hated Steelers. I remember freezing at the first Super Bowl held outdoors in the North, Super Bowl XLVIII in East Rutherford, New Jersey, but that's just because I'm too used to living in Florida. The scene was beautiful, and it was a wonderful tribute to the Mara family, who'd been so generous to the NFL for more than half a century. And thank you, Les Moonves of CBS, who decided to change Super Bowl L to Super Bowl 50, which looked so much better and saved every broadcaster, writer, and fan from either being confused or having to look it up.

CHAPTER 19

One player who won three Super Bowls is among my favorites for a different reason. Very few men have both served in the military and played in the NFL. The names that come to mind, of course, are Roger Staubach, Rocky Bleier, and Joe Bellino, who was on a ship in the blockade during the Cuban Missile Crisis and also commanded a minesweeper in Vietnam.

But one man, former Dallas Cowboys defensive tackle Chad Hennings, won three championships and flew forty-five combat missions over Iraq and Turkey. He said his time at the Air Force Academy helped shape the man he is today, a man who put off playing in the NFL for five years so he could fulfill his commitment to his country. Every Memorial Day, we should salute Hennings and everyone who has given us their protection and pride, along with their families.

"We don't talk enough about character in this country," Hennings said to me one time. "Our culture tells too many of us that we are victims, that we have no control over our surroundings. But we do have a choice in the way we live, in the way we act."

The way Hennings lived has its roots in the small community of Elberon, Iowa, where his dad was a farmer and twelve hundred cattle had to be fed every day. There were a total of 194 people in Elberon; the closest neighbor was miles away. Trick-or-treating on Halloween meant going to the nearest small town, some ten miles down the road. "My dad taught my brothers and sister that someone had to feed and take care of the livestock," said Hennings, who now has two college-age kids of his own. "We learned responsibility at an early age."

I'd imagine most boys would love to fly jets and play for the Dallas Cowboys. But not many make that dream come true. In high school, Hennings was big and fast and recruited by Big Ten schools, but he wanted more of a challenge. He chose the Air Force Academy and the great coach Fisher DeBerry. Under DeBerry, the Falcons always won the Commander-in-Chief's Trophy, the triangular rivalry against Army and Navy. DeBerry won it fourteen times in his twenty-one seasons. "We'd start singing, 'Off we go, into the wild blue yonder' as soon as the game ended."

And then Hennings did.

Barely fitting in the cockpit at six foot four, Hennings flew A-10 jets, called Warthogs for the unattractive design of the powerful plane with a Gatling gun—the forerunner of the modern machine gun—attached to its nose that could fire off four thousand bullets a minute. Climbing high into the sun, Hennings said that he yearned for the NFL, but nothing was better than being a brother-in-arms.

"I was actually drafted by Tom Landry, but I never got to play for him," said Hennings, who graduated in 1988. "I finished my service obligation in 1992, flew back from the base in London, and went to try out for Jimmy

Johnson and Gil Brandt in the same day. They liked what they saw and I became a Cowboy."

It also meant that, within one calendar year, Hennings flew combat missions and played in a Super Bowl. The Cowboys beat Buffalo that year, 52–17, in Super Bowl XXVII in Pasadena. Hennings stood on the sideline and looked up as the traditional flyover zoomed past. "It was emotional for me," said Hennings. "The lessons I learned in the military, about character and morality and taking care of your brothers, can never be replaced. It didn't make dealing with Charles Haley or Michael Irvin all that difficult."

Hennings has the greatest admiration for those who've come home from the military without an arm or a leg, yet somehow find the courage to continue their service. "We don't do enough for veterans," said Hennings, who's written a book, *The Forces of Character*, that deals with building a life of impact. "Veterans don't want a handout. They want to be useful to society. And they need our support."

So let's remember to toast those who have guarded us, and make it our mission to honor their mission.

CHAPTER 20

I n my wild and privileged career, I've covered more than thirty-five Final Fours—all seven of the Indianapolis tournaments. I've been lucky to see Jack Morris go the distance when the Twins beat the Braves in 1991 in the deafening Metrodome, and to witness the Red Sox, with thirteen third strikes to use, lose to the New York Mets in

With former NCAA champion, New York Knick, and television analyst Greg Anthony at the 2016 Final Four in Houston

Reporting from the 2012 NCAA Regional Final in Boston

With Coach Gary Williams at the 2001 Final Four

the World Series after Carter, Mitchell, and Knight singled and Mookie Wilson dribbled one past Bill Buckner for the ages. Each event has had its own color and drama, even the blowouts.

Working in sports for four decades means there's just about no one in the Final Four broadcasts I haven't worked with, so I'll start with Hall of Famer Dick Enberg. I met Dick in 1980, at the first Final Four I covered in Indianapolis. He was working at NBC back then, part of the great trio with Billy Packer and Al McGuire. I was a young writer and our conversation wasn't very long; we talked about the teams, but I'll never forget he ended it with, "So, Lesley, what are you reading?" It was so emblematic of Dick, who's been associated with academics as long as he's been at Rose Bowls or Wimbledon.

The pride of Mount Clemens, Michigan, a town of two thousand people, Dick told me his hometown was best known for the time Mae West came to sample the mineral waters at the bath house. It wasn't a rich community. Dick grew up in a drafty two-story farmhouse with no indoor plumbing. But that's part of the beauty, the dignity, of my journey: working with people who grew up in a farming community in eastern Michigan or the streets of New York City. Dick has his shirts made on Bond Street in London, but his voice is pure Midwest.

John Madden taught me the most, but Al Michaels might have been the most entertaining. Without a filter, he always said what he thought and he didn't care who was listening. After a World Series game in Cleveland, Tim McCarver, Al Michaels, and I got in the stretch limousine to go back to the hotel, and Al took a swig of the Johnnie Walker Blue he'd ordered for himself. Not knowing what to say or do, I commented, "Wow, Greg Maddux had great stuff."

Al looked at me, annoyed. "Lezley, Lezley, Lezley," he said, in the nasal way he pronounced my name, "after the game, we don't talk baseball, we *rip* people!"

Al was a riot, as talented as anyone, and I'm talking about a group that includes Curt Gowdy and Vin Scully and Pat Summerall. I did almost every sport with Al: *Monday Night Football*, the World Series, and the Triple Crown. He was a joy, never leaving anyone hanging or unsure of where the broadcast was going. The great Charles Osgood once said, "TV is like a duck on the pond—he looks placid

on the surface, but he's paddling furiously underneath."
The first generation of television broadcasters that I knew
were all giants: Marv Albert, Dick Stockton, Bob Costas,
Michaels, Madden, and Summerall, Enberg, Jack Buck,
Verne Lunquist, and Pat O'Brien. The next generation—
James Brown, Jim Nantz, Joe Buck, Greg Gumbel, and Ian
Eagle—are equally as talented.

One of my favorite moments with Enberg was during
the NCAA tournament in 2001, when Dick, Bill Walton,
and I were covering Arizona in the regional final. Bill's
son Luke had just one turnover but Bill was brutal:
"Walton, Walton—that's a terrrribbble pass!" Enberg had
to play the father. "Now, now, Bill, he's just a young man,

With colleague and great friend Jim Nantz at a CBS event in 2009

With Jim Nantz

he's doing the best he can." My journey has been full of these moments.

At the Final Four in 1980, I was in my twenties, and at my last one in Indianapolis, I was in my sixties—what a wonderful ride it's been. In 1980, I remember thinking how strange it was that Larry Brown, who'd played for the great Dean Smith at Carolina and now coaches at UCLA, lost the final to Denny Crum (remember the "Doctors of Dunk" with Darrell Griffith?). Crum, of course, had played for Wooden at UCLA. It was such a strange circle of relationships. One afternoon, I went with a group of writers to Hinkle Fieldhouse (this was six years before the movie *Hoosiers*!). We saw an East–West All-Star game, and I remember being stunned at the building.

The bleachers at Hinkle were from 1928, one year after the Palestra was built, but the space seemed so much bigger. The final game was held at Market Square Arena— long gone now—but that was when the Final Four held smaller crowds. Attending the Final Four, you would see everyone in the lobby or in the local bars—coaches, assistants, trainers, even high school administrators. I remember everybody wore a warm-up suit (they still do) and you'd call everyone "Coach," even if you couldn't remember his name.

Coaches were characters back then, and the Big East ruled the country. Invented by Commissioner and Coach Dave Gavitt of Providence in 1979, the league was formed to pull in the big TV markets: Georgetown in Washington,

With radio legend Mike Francesa and broadcaster Pat O'Brien at the 1995 Final Four

Boston College in Boston, Villanova in Philadelphia, St. John's in New York. Football was not even a consideration. By 1983, the league was playing its conference championship in Madison Square Garden and the party was on. The Big East was rough and raw (was there ever a more electrifying point guard than Pearl Washington, or a center as terrifying as Patrick Ewing?), and, unlike now, the coaches actually hung around together. Every summer, Jim Boeheim (Syracuse), Bill Raftery (Seton Hall), maybe three other coaches, and a couple of guys from the league would go to Ireland to play golf. Raftery said he once borrowed Boeheim's shoes and they "whined all the way up the fairway."

The league and the people were a blast. Coaches like Lou Carnesecca of St. John's would tell his players not to get too high on themselves: "Today a peacock, tomorrow a feather duster." Rollie Massimino of Villanova looked like a shaken bottle of seltzer water, all rumpled and wild. When people used to ask me why I did what I did, I'd say, "Villanova 66, Georgetown 64"—that was the title score in 1985, considered one of the biggest upsets in the history of college basketball. Two years ago, when Villanova again won the national title (this time under Jay Wright, who'd been Rollie Massimino's assistant), I told Jay he should patent the phrase "It ain't ova 'til it's Villanova!"

I've always thought that America blooms during March Madness—brackets, spoilers, fantasy, favorites—and everyone is involved. It's spring, a great time of optimism in America, and almost everyone either went to college,

Interviewing North Carolina coach Roy Williams at the 2015 Final Four (he's been to nine of them!)

or roots for a local team. I loved when George Mason made a run in 2006, beating Connecticut in overtime in the regional finals in Washington. We all thought George Mason was the architect of the Bill of Rights and then, all of sudden, that was the team we loved in the Final Four. Nineteen eighty was considered the birth of the modern era (any number of at-large teams could qualify, not just one team from one league, like the ACC, where Carolina was always the representative, or, rarely, NC State). Teams were seeded in a bracket and a committee convened to discuss it. That year was also when the last third-place team played a game, which turned out to be Purdue over Iowa.

In 1991, Duke had been considered the Buffalo Bills of the Final Four—always there, but always on the losing end. But that year was magical. The Blue Devils beat UNLV in the semifinals, 79–77. I had the assignment for CBS of reporting from behind both benches, which is not allowed anymore, but I remember Jerry Tarkanian chewing on his towel and yelling at his team in the Hoosier Dome, "We're playing like *they're* the defending champion!" People then were just learning to spell "Krzyzewski." It was also a bizarre Final Four because Dean Smith, a model of decorum (he made his players know the history of civil rights, and he never publicly lost his cool), got thrown out of the semifinals. Even stranger, it happened against Kansas and his former assistant Roy Williams, who idolized Coach Smith. Kansas beat Carolina, 79–73. Then Duke beat Kansas in the final by seven points, and went on to win the *next* championship in 1992 (beating Michigan in Minneapolis). Those back-to-back titles were historic, but the Blue Devils didn't win another championship until they went back to Indianapolis in 2010, when Gordon Hayward's prayer of a shot for Butler just upped out at the buzzer, 61–59.

In between those two Duke titles, Arizona beat defending champion Kentucky in overtime at the RCA Dome (no longer the Hoosier Dome) in 1997. Before an overwhelming Kentucky crowd, I looked at the Arizona Wildcats and I remember thinking that this is how some day America might be viewed—a blend of black, white, and Hispanic. Just think of that team: Bibby, Strawberry, Miles Simon—all from different backgrounds and colors. It was a beautiful sight to see.

Coach Tom Izzo, now considered one of the greatest coaches in history, won his first title in 2000, in Indianapolis. In the RCA Dome, his Spartans beat Florida, and who knew that Gator coach Billy Donovan, who seemed so young and innocent, would go on to win back-to-back titles, one of them in Indy? Billy the Kid, who'd been Pitino's last scholarship player at Providence, had his revenge in the RCA Dome in 2006, when Florida beat UCLA, 74–57, behind the brilliant play of Joakim Noah.

In 2015, Duke won the title again in Indy—does Coach K have a home there yet? Once more he was in Lucas Oil Stadium, when his Blue Devils, behind freshman point guard Tyus Jones, beat Wisconsin 68–63. Coach K's now won five titles, three of them in Indianapolis. What is

With Duke and US Olympic basketball coach Mike Krzyzewski

it about Indianapolis? It wasn't that Coach K loved the Indy 500, or the Indianapolis Colts (he's from Chicago), or hung out with Reggie Miller. It wasn't that he ate dinner every night at St. Elmo's (okay, maybe he did), but it was because, with each of those teams, he learned how to adapt. That's Krzyzewski's brilliance. He knows what it takes to win. He takes that philosophy to the Olympic Games. And he wins there, too.

You can make the argument that five Duke titles today might compete with Wooden's ten, but Krzyzewski will shoot you down. He claims that would be for all of us to say, not him. Personally, I think Coach K, Pitino, Jay Wright, Izzo, and John Calipari round out my top five, with John Beilein and Bill Self right behind. Brad Stevens and Donovan left the college game, or they'd be there, too. I know this is a long way from seeing seven titles in Indy, but my opinions are on the table. What do you think?

CHAPTER 21

There are lots of things young women should know. They should know how to dream and that dreams come true. They should know that prejudice isn't pretty, but smiling is. They should challenge themselves and also those around them. And they should do the right thing. I loved Billie Jean King and Arthur Ashe and many of the people I worked with. I also let people lead me places I didn't need to go. Like my hair.

I really wanted to call this book *Hair-anoia*, but everyone told me it wouldn't sell. My first struggles with my hair came in tenth grade, when I would wrap my long brown shank around a giant Hi-C can to make it straight. Ironing came next, which meant arranging my hair on the ironing board while hoping not to burn my neck. This was the 1970s, when everyone wanted to look like Cher.

It was a cool time in America. Alan Shepard hit a golf ball on the moon and *Jesus Christ Superstar* opened on Broadway. Doctors Without Borders was invented by some French physicians, which went on to inspire Basketball Without Borders, run by my friend Kim Bohuny, vice president of international operations for the NBA. *A Clockwork Orange* was *the* complicated, popular movie. Back in 1971, the voting age had been reduced to eighteen, my age, and I went to work for Senator George McGovern, the Democratic candidate for president. We sang along to the Stones' "Wild Horses" while tossing our long hair behind our backs, and Clint Eastwood made us hip quoting him in *Dirty Harry*. Evonne Goolagong, the coolest of the cool, won Wimbledon, and the Cowboys won the Super Bowl.

I went off to Boston College and didn't think about my hair again until 1975, when, while working at the *Globe*, I got a curly, sexy permanent. Or so I thought. *Time* magazine had named "women" its "Person of the Year" and I wanted to get in on the deal. I guess instead of looking like a wavy Linda Ronstadt, I looked more like an English sheepdog, and Vince Doria, my sports editor, said to me, and I quote, "You are not going on the road representing the *Boston Globe* until that grows out."

Mortified, I said, "You're kidding."

"No, you look like you've been on the back of a motor-cycle for four days."

Since then, I've tried everything—and you can see from the pictures that more than forty years in the public eye has meant a lot of different hairdos. When Chris Evert won Wimbledon, I went back to chin length and straight, but I looked more like Duane Allman than a tennis champion. President Jimmy Carter admitted he'd "committed adultery in his heart," but I don't think he had me in mind. My friends and I would pretend to be Charlie's Angels, and I always had to be Kate Jackson, the smart one with the crummy hair. That was 1976, the year I had to wait outside Three Rivers Stadium in the freezing cold to talk to quarterback Terry Bradshaw. With my notepad and my pen in the freezing cold, my hair was plastered to my head.

When I first went to CBS, they would send me to a big-cheese hairdresser to get my hair "fixed." His name was John Sahag, and his salon was on Madison Avenue in New York. He was known for styling celebrities, from Sarah Jessica Parker to Demi Moore and—I'm not making this up—he'd cut your hair while it was dry and you were standing up. There wasn't any music and no one spoke, in case it interrupted his vision. Of course, cutting my skinny strands could not have been much of a challenge, and all I wanted to do, anyway, was talk to him about his life. He'd been born in Beirut, raised in Australia, and learned to cut hair in Paris. Sahag (pronounced, of course, "Sa-haagh") knew nothing about sports and I'm sure I bored him. He once told me he didn't cut hair, he "felt it." It cost CBS a fortune and I looked pretty much the same when I walked out as when I had walked in.

I finally gave up and let everyone try everything. CBS had a wonderful hairdresser who we called "Mare with the Hair." She did her best. When I went to ABC, they sent me to another superstar hairdresser. Frédéric Fekkai was known as the "mane man," and his salon on Fifth Avenue was as glorious as the one in Palm Beach. He loved women and bone structure and could envision strong winds blowing through Cindy Crawford's hair. Of course, she was a client. My experience with him was limited—twice he canceled on me, once for Jessica Lange and once for Claudia Schiffer. I can't say I blame him.

And so it went, until one time, at the World Figure Skating Championships in 1999, the great Peggy Fleming

With Olympic great Peggy Fleming, with whom I traveled the world for eight years

called me in my room and said, "You've got to come down to the lobby right now." I hurried downstairs. I thought maybe she didn't feel well. She sat me down on the couch and said, "Oh dear, oh dear—there's a website about your hair." The internet wasn't that big then, and we didn't really pay attention to it, but Peggy was a sweetheart and thought I ought to know. It's why I tell all young women never to Google themselves. They aren't going to like it. I told Peggy that from then on, she would have to stand behind me, hiding behind my back and draping her hair over my shoulders. Okay, that didn't work. It's why I used to love being assigned a cold weather game in Green Bay

With Hall of Fame trainer Wayne Lukas in Saratoga

or Chicago, where I could wear a hat, or the Kentucky Derby, where I could wear a *really* big hat.

When I went back to CBS, the woman with the world's most perfect hair, Jen Sabatelle, had been promoted in communications, taking over for the great LeslieAnne Wade. I had met Jen many years before when she worked in a restaurant on the Upper East Side, and I thought she was a doll. Little did I know that I would be working with her and that hair every day. She would try to torture me by throwing her glossy locks around. One year, she got highlights and it looked even better. I didn't speak to her for a week. Now that I'm older and a blonde (what, you didn't notice?), I'm at peace. Well, until last year, when I was at baggage claim in Dallas and a guy yelled out from across the room, "Hey, you know what? You look like an older Lesley Visser!" Sigh.

CHAPTER 22

Carpool Karaoke is the funniest bit on TV, when *The Late Late Show* host James Corden and a famous singer drive around and have an old-fashioned sing-along. Actually, his name is wrong—it should be James Car-don, since his best stuff is behind the seat belt with the radio on. But after that, it's perfect, and it's also a riot that, as far as sports, he roots for West Ham, the English Premier League team that never finishes higher than fifth and is known for a group of skinny standing-room-only pimply lads who sing "I'm Forever Blowing Bubbles" while yelling at the opposition.

I wish there were a sports version, so here's my idea. Most actors want to be athletes, and most athletes want to be rock stars. Maybe Corden could recruit some athletes to become semi-famous singers. We mix the best of the best, from Dwyane Wade to Kobe and LeBron, to Steph Curry and Kevin Durant, to Russell Wilson and Troy Aikman, to J. J. Watt and Colin Kaepernick, to Sidney Crosby and Alex Ovechkin, to Mike Trout, Mike Piazza, and American Pharoah. We have them sing their favorite songs about sports, while Ellen DeGeneres dances off to the side and the Roots keep the beat. It will be a mixture of walk-up songs, rap, and hip-hop, plus blues and rock and roll. People will laugh and sing along. What's better than that? Obviously, I haven't totally fleshed this out, so I'm open to suggestions.

Here are my favorite sports songs—can we get Cam Newton or Phil Mickelson to sing along with James Car-don?

"Start Me Up" (The Packers played this as they took the field.)

"Sweet Caroline" ("So-good, so-good!")

"Enter Sandman" (In other words, "You're out!")

"Let's Get It Started" (Forget the Black Eyed Peas' Super Bowl appearance, this is great for a crowd-rouser.)

"*Monday Night Football* Theme" (The old Hank Williams version.)

"Lose Yourself" (Even Eminem has to dance around.)

"The Star-Spangled Banner" (It can't be played enough.)

"Roar" (Katy Perry—this one's for the girls.)

"We Are the Champions" (Rare, but can't help falling in love.)

"Eye of the Tiger" (Survivor had it right.)

"One Shining Moment" (The best song ever, not just sports. Besides my two favorites . . .)

"Fly Me to The Moon" and "Wee Small Hours of The Morning" (By Ol' Blue Eyes. These are the best. I defy anyone not to get jammed up on seeing the crowning of the NCAA national basketball champion on CBS, with the confetti swirling around, getting in Jim Nantz's hair, and everyone singing along . . . "The ball is tipped . . . and there you are . . . you're running for your life, you're a shooting star." See? I'm emotional already . . .)

CHAPTER 23

O f course I was nervous. I had experienced enormous challenges—presenting the Lombardi Trophy, being the first woman analyst for the NFL in both radio (on Westwood One) and TV (for the Miami Dolphins). I'd even carried the 2004 Olympic torch (celebrating the 100th

Carrying the Olympic torch in New York before the 2004 Olympiad in Athens

Being enshrined in the Pro Football Hall of Fame in 2006. Photo by Amy Glanzman.

anniversary of the modern Games in Athens) because the International Olympic Committee had called me "a pioneer and standard-bearer." (By the way, it isn't actually the torch that goes around the world, but the flame. There are even two airplanes to keep the flame lit as it crosses an ocean, and I got to take the flame up Sixth Avenue in New York and carry it to Central Park, where my friends all met me and we went to the Essex House to celebrate.)

But this night in Canton, Ohio, was different. As I sat on the dais among the seven Hall of Fame inductees, while listening to my friend Al Michaels talk about my career, I had doubts about whether I'd be able to speak.

My mind began to wander. It was hard not to be overwhelmed in the moment, something I won't allow myself to do when I'm interviewing an athlete or a coach. Dan Dierdorf, in that wonderful baritone voice, had told me to write my speech down. He said, "When you're enshrined in the Pro Football Hall of Fame, you won't be able to remember everything or everybody, so put it down on paper."

I remember hoping that I'd worn the right clothes that night. The other honorees were inducted wearing a gold blazer—the deliberate symbol of the "gold standard" they represent to the game of professional football. With the help of a girlfriend, I'd settled on a light pink St. John jacket. I hoped it was symbolic, strong but still feminine. I think it fit my personality. But Dierdorf telling me to write it down was the best advice I'd received since my mother told me more than forty years earlier to "cross when it says 'don't walk.'" She would have been so proud.

Many friends came to Canton and many flowers arrived. I got notes from people like Marv Levy and Gregg Popovich and Romeo Crennel, all people I'd admired. Canton is a perfect place—the Pro Football Hall of Fame is even shaped like a football. The whole experience makes you happy. There was a parade the day before the enshrinement. Each inductee had a convertible with a driver, so I sat high on the back as the car meandered through downtown Canton. Hundreds of people lined the streets—John Madden, Troy Aikman, and Harry Carson got the biggest cheers. I was thrilled just to have my name on the side of the car.

The Pro Football Hall of Fame in Canton, a small town of 70,000, is tucked away in the northeast corner of Ohio. Some people might wonder how this working-class town ever became the home of pro football immortality. There were three reasons:

- The American Professional Football Association, later renamed the National Football League, was founded in Canton on September 17, 1920.
- The Canton Bulldogs were an early-day pro football power, even before the days of the NFL. They were also the first two-time champion of the NFL, in 1922 and 1923. The great Olympian Jim Thorpe, the first big-name athlete to play pro football, played it for the first time with the Bulldogs beginning in 1915.
- Canton citizens rallied and organized themselves in the early 1960s and launched a determined campaign to earn their city the honor of housing pro football's Hall of Fame.

So it was kind of surreal to hear Al Michaels talk about my career that day, August 5, 2006, when I became the first woman ever recognized by the Professional Football Hall of Fame with the Pete Rozelle Radio-Television Award. I joined Dallas Cowboys quarterback Troy Aikman, feared Giants linebacker Harry Carson, good friend John Madden, prolific quarterback Warren Moon, the great Packer Reggie White, and the Cowboys offensive lineman Rayfield Wright. I was proud to hear Al's words, and I hoped the late Pete Rozelle would have appreciated the meaning of me winning his award. Do you believe in miracles? Yes, it was almost unimaginable, and my mind drifted to the historic names that reside in Canton—George "Papa Bear" Halas, Roger Staubach, Jim Otto, Marcus Allen, Raymond Berry, Terry Bradshaw, Mean Joe Greene, Earl Campbell, Frank Gifford, Bart Starr, Bronko Nagurski, Ray Nitschke, and hundreds of others. I thought about the esteemed broadcasters, journalists, and past recipients of the Pete Rozelle Award that I would join in the broadcasting wing—Jack Buck, Pat Summerall, Curt Gowdy Sr., who called the Red Sox games of my youth, Dick Enberg, and Roone Arledge. ROONE ARLEDGE for crying out loud!

I had been thinking of all of this when my time to speak was approaching. I was in awe when Al Michaels called my name. Among the hundreds of well-wishers and friends, even the unapproachable Al Davis spoke with me that weekend. And Troy Aikman, who was at the top of the list among the stars inducted that year, mentioned me in his speech: "Lesley was a pioneer in her profession. She was one of the first women to cover the sport and she really knows the game. It makes me proud to be in her company today." He winked at me as he said it. I nearly fainted. Dan Marino, another Hall of Famer and my CBS Sports colleague at the time, said, "You can tell that Lesley has a real love of the game of football. She has a passion for the personalities and for the people who play the game."

Dan nailed it. I love the game. I had wanted to cover sports from the time I was ten years old. The significance of being the first woman in the Pro Football Hall of Fame is that today women can do anything they want to do. My entire career came about because of my love of sports. I never

On the field with Hall of Fame great Dan Marino at a 2014 Miami Dolphins game

for one second set out for the money or the fame. Being the first woman in Canton is stunning because I started out like everybody else—I just loved sports. It's funny when I look back. At one point in my career I described myself as "a hardcore football, basketball, baseball guy . . ." It makes me laugh when I think about it. I always said there are two kinds of women who do this for a living: women who love sports and end up on television, and women who want to be on television and end up in sports. After a while, you can tell which is which. John Madden wrote me a beautiful note before the ceremony that contained words I often repeat when I speak in public. It said, "You can't be born into the Hall of Fame, you can't buy your way into the Hall of Fame, you have to earn it."

CHAPTER 24

The biggest change I've seen over four decades of covering sports is that everyone has become a citizen journalist. Maybe "journalist" is too strong a word. Because of Twitter and Facebook and talk radio, everyone has an opinion, well thought out or not.

That's the trouble with Twitter. For all its good, it can be an unaccountable venue for racist or ethnic hate, most often with no name attached. Former Miami Dolphin Brent Grimes must be sorry his wife has access to Twitter—she recently tweeted that Dolphin owner Stephen Ross "and his jew [sic] buddies" should not have cut her husband. The internet is a breakthrough in worldwide freedom, but it doesn't give you or me or anyone the right to bully or be unkind. And it seems to be harder on women. I tell many young women not to Google themselves or search on Twitter, that they aren't going to like what they read, much of it anonymous, because it's going to make them feel crummy. Facebook has much to admire, but it, too, can be a place of self-indulgence, of mini-me selfies and personal glorification. I don't think Mother Teresa posted too many selfies. As habits change, new media is supported by the shifting winds of advertising. As recently as 2011, advertisers spent no money on mobile devices; now they spend more than $77 billion per year! Digital is poised to pass TV in ad spending, and the *Wall Street Journal* says that media companies who ignore YouTube or Snapchat do so at their peril. We're not in Kansas anymore.

One time, actress Scarlett Johansson was asked why she is never in the gossip pages or snapping selfies at every event. She answered that "silence is money." She didn't mean financial success, but emotional gold. I've found that less time on social media has meant more focus on my work. Which has nothing to do with excitement.

Although there are apps that never would have been around ten years ago, many are worth a peek or two. One is from sack-master Super Bowl MVP Von Miller, when he was on *Dancing with the Stars*. He tells you *exactly* how to move your feet. I come from an era where dancing meant just kind of shuffling around, not really making eye contact. But this app from Miller shows you precisely what to do, how to move left or right, where to slow down and where to turn it up, how to really project yourself. Wanna dance?

Salaries and franchise valuations have also changed radically. I just read that a nice house in 1960 cost $8,500; now the same house costs $450,000. It's no different with sports franchises. The Dallas Cowboys haven't won the Super Bowl since 1995, and haven't been to the NFC Championship since then. Yet when *Forbes* released its annual list of the most valuable sports teams in the world, number one was Dallas, with a value of over $4 billion! It means that being slightly better than mediocre in a league followed almost exclusively in America is now worth more than Manchester United in England ($3.32

billion), Barcelona ($3.55 billion), or Real Madrid ($3.65 billion), all hugely successful global teams. The laughingstock of the NBA, the New York Knicks, were the most valuable NBA team, at $3 billion, but at least the NBA is known throughout China and Africa.

The biggest difference can be summed up in one sentence: Tom Brady has a cookbook! That's right. Tom Brady! For $200, those of you wealthy enough to buy this book (which he calls a "living document") can learn how to make Japanese-style fish cakes or use only a spoonful of lime juice in your eggs. When I started covering the NFL more than four decades ago, I'd meet a quarterback for some pizza and a beer. Twenty years later, I remember going to the apartment of Zach Thomas, who was rooming with fellow Dolphin rookie Larry Izzo. They had half-empty Chinese food cartons all over the living room and pizza boxes near the TV. Brett Favre, in his second year, had Cajun chicken on the counter and six-packs of Schlitz in the refrigerator. Yet I read that in 2015, Shon Coleman of Auburn had banana shakes for breakfast and Cali rolls (huh?—some combination of cucumber and crab) for lunch. How times have changed.

And it isn't just the food. The William Morris Agency, with offices from Sydney to London to L.A. and New York, bought and merged with IMG (full disclosure—I love that phrase in the movies—I've been with IMG for more than thirty years). The combined company, WME/IMG, then paid $4 billion for the rights to the Ultimate Fighting Championship. You read that right—$4 billion! Apparently Ari Emanuel and Patrick Whitesell—the über power brokers from William Morris—knew something we didn't: that the UFC is rising faster on the global sports landscape than the NFL and golf combined. It took the NFL forty years to overtake baseball and horse racing as the biggest sport in America, but it might take the UFC about ten minutes. I didn't watch the UFC before, but now that it's in more than 150 countries, it's going to be on in my house.

Two other big changes in my lifetime have been Twitter and Facebook, which too often is a place of mini-me—pictures of people and their friends and not enough topical discussion.

Magazines were enormously popular forty years ago, and the slow demise of *Sports Illustrated* and *The Sporting News* has led to the rise of internet sites like Deadspin and The Big Lead. These aren't necessarily funny or filled with deep thought, but they are quick and opinionated. In a strange irony, people are starting to think deeply about concussions, yet cage fighting is at its most popular. With everyone as a commentator—microphone or not—stories stretch on for weeks and even months. Tom Brady agreed to sit out the first four games of the 2016 season, but that didn't stop Twitter. Here were some of the reactions. "No, no, Brady should take the case all the way to the Supreme Court," "Tom, Tom, go out swinging," "This is nonsense, take it like a man," "The federal judge who threw out the appeal is the one who should be punished," "Long enough, put this one to bed," "Admit it Brady, you're not bigger than the brand." This went on for weeks, and not one comment had a name assigned.

Being loud and brash even has its advantages. Bill Simmons wrote a column in 1999 for his personal site,

"Boston Sports Guy," in which he called the ESPYs a "TV holocaust." The column was forwarded to Bristol, read by many, and eventually the company offered him a job. His "brand" has continued to grow, although I don't think he would, as he did in that column, make fat lesbian jokes about Rosie O'Donnell when she presented a lifetime achievement award to Billie Jean King. On second thought, maybe he would. There's nothing phony about Bill Simmons.

Another gigantic shift in the culture of sports has been the dominance of talk radio. When I first went to the Super Bowl thirty-five years ago and was a guest on Radio Row, it was really a row. One row, with maybe five stations. Now "radio row" commands an entire convention center, and there are hosts from Japan and London and every small station from sea to shining sea. The first sports talk radio I remember was called "the Sports Huddle": three loudmouths from Boston who were hysterically funny and didn't care what anyone thought. In 1969, the Sports Huddle was at the very end of the AM dial, and none of them worked full-time in radio, so they didn't care about satisfying advertisers. The legendary center of the group was 250-pound real estate developer Eddie Andelman, whose chin hit his breastbone because, as he said, "the Andelmans have no necks." Mark Witkin was a lawyer and Jim McCarthy an insurance consultant. As Witkin once said, "Not only do we represent the fans, we are the fans." They were originals, paying their way into every event and intimidating anyone in their path. Witkin was the only outsider, born in Pennsylvania and the closest thing to a moderator when the discussion went off the rails, which was about every other minute.

They took calls, and that was the best part of the show: someone from Chicago complaining about the Cubs or the Blackhawks. The Three Musketeers either *did* know everything about everything, or acted like they did. They owned the time slot, beating all the competition, and still refused to sell out. One hot dog company offered them $5,000 (big radio money back then) to put their faces on frankfurter packages. Andelman, Witkin, and McCarthy laughed it off. Then they made their own products, like "Ice Cream of the Week," which might be strawberry salami or chocolate lobster roll. It was hard to tell the spoof from the serious—one time they gave out free T-shirts to anyone who could sing "Take Me Out to the Ball Game" in another language. More than thirty-five people called in. Another bit they did was called "the Sam Huff school of piling on."

Don't you wish sports talk radio were like that today? Some shows are a riot. *Mike and Mike* makes you laugh, as did Mike Francesca when he was on with Chris Russo. All the Boston guys are funny. There are two in Miami, Jeff DeForrest and John "Footy" Kross, who are original and laugh-out-loud funny. "The Fabulous Sports Babe" in Tampa, Nanci Donnellan, always makes me smile. In New York, the iconic Bill Mazer had the first sports talk show, back in 1964. Then WFAN had the first *all*-sports programming in 1987. In between, WSOU, a tiny but talented station at Seton Hall University, began a call-in show back in 1965. In 2015, they celebrated their fiftieth anniversary. Sports talk radio is all day, all night, all week,

Guesting on great friend Tony Kornheiser's radio/TV show

all year. A friend of mine from Miami, Charlie Brown (his real name), drives home to Chicago and picks up sports talk radio the whole way—from "The Game" in Orlando, to CBS outside Atlanta, to "The Zone" in Nashville, up to "The Score" in Chicago. He used to listen to Joe B. Hall and Denny Crum out of WKYU in Kentucky, but the show was canceled three years ago.

The good and bad of sports talk radio is that, to the good, it gets every opinion out there and leaves little room for hiding prejudice. To the bad, it's often screaming, huffing and puffing, and ready to blow the house down. Hopefully, the wide world of sports is starting to come full circle. When I started, Arthur Ashe and Bud Collins went to South Africa to try and change apartheid.

Muhammad Ali was a conscientious objector. In July 2016, LeBron James, Dwyane Wade, and others called for athletes to engage in conversation about blacks and whites, to talk about social change. LeBron stressed that black lives matter, but so do white. Charles Barkley said that most black crime is black on black and that African Americans have to respect *themselves* first. He added that police brutality is not to be tolerated and must be investigated. It's positive that people are talking. Maybe

In Doha, Qatar, with Olympic gold medalists Nancy Hogshead-Makar and Donna de Varona

decades from now, we'll see the impact of having had the first African American president and the first female presidential candidate from a major party.

One of the other big changes I've seen is Title IX. Passed in 1972, it really came of age at the Atlanta Olympics in 1996, when the young women of Title IX won everything—soccer, softball, basketball, and gymnastics—the first time ever that the United States won the team gold. The U.S. women ruled those games. And the opportunities created by Billie Jean King were no less than those created by Jackie Robinson, it's just that as a society we gravitate toward the men. When asked who the greatest tennis player in history is, at least we can argue Serena or Steffi, along with Roger Federer and Rod Laver.

Many other women are powering all kinds of success, and that's what we need to celebrate: the mother who makes a difference, the teacher, Ellen DeGeneres, Tina Fey, Viola Davis, the female boss who promotes younger women. Aristotle said that "educating the mind without educating the heart is no education at all." In the end, only kindness matters. I'm not great on infrastructure or technology; I hope you will teach me. You might be younger, but I see you. I hope you see me. And if you are older, you must know, you're not too old and it's not too late. And thank you, Les Moonves and Sean McManus from CBS, for starting the first national show of all women talking sports, which includes veterans like Dara Torres, Andrea Kremer, Amy Trask, Laila Ali, Tracy Wolfson, Katrina Adams, Dana Jacobson, Summer Sanders, Allie LaForce, and Swin Cash. We need to talk. And we definitely need to listen.

BEARS 2005
GAME ONE
CBS
CBS SPORTS
PRESS BOX
PACKERS
NFL
DIVISION
LESLEY VISSER
CBS SPORTS
PRESS BOX
GAME 6
LAMBEAU FIELD 50 Years 1957-2007
AUTHORIZED BY
Lesley Visser
CBS
Sept 21, 2008
NAME
AFFILIATION
DATE
AUTOGRAPHS
SUNDAY NOVEM
10819
6500

CHAPTER 25

I had the blessing of having a passion—actually two. I loved sports and I loved journalism. I'm a natural reporter, born of observation and curiosity. I can read anything. And I mean anything. From how the universe exploded to the Orioles' brilliant pitching staff of 1971 (recited by Amy Adams in *Trouble with the Curve*, although she mispronounced "Mike Cuellar"). The renowned poet Ralph Waldo Emerson said, "Nothing great can be accomplished without enthusiasm." Know that anything and everything is open to you. Another great poet, William Blake, put it best in his poem "The Tyger," from *Songs of Innocence and Experience,* often quoted by my mother: "On what wings dare he aspire? What the hand, dare seize the fire?"

Most of my earliest lessons came from books that made an enormous impact on me as a child—*The Jungle Book* by Rudyard Kipling, where all the animals, with no anger, went to the "peace trough" during the dry season (why can't we have that now?), and especially the Winnie-the-Pooh series by A. A. Milne. My favorite was *When We Were Very Young*, which had wonderful poetry and profound secret messages. In "Halfway Down," Milne writes:

Halfway down the stairs
is a stair
where i sit . . .
i'm not at the bottom,
i'm not at the top . . .
And all sorts of funny thoughts
Run round my head.
It isn't really
Anywhere!
It's somewhere else
Instead!

Once you realize that anywhere you go, there you are, you'll be comfortable in your skin. And the book teaches us that no one is any greater than anyone else. In "Teddy Bear," Milne writes about Winnie-the-Pooh meeting the chubby King of France, called the "Handsome King." Pooh couldn't believe it, a fat king considered stately and dignified! Pooh asked,

"Are you . . . by any chance
His Majesty the King of France?"
The other answered, "I am that,"
Bowed stiffly and removed his hat;
Then he said, "Excuse me," with an air,
"But is it Mr. Edward Bear?"
And Teddy, bending very low
Replied politely, "Even so!"

Perfect.

Everything interests me, but nothing as much as a great game, either in person or on TV. My husband and I were in Norway this summer when France beat Germany—the world's greatest soccer team—in the semis of Euro 2016. The continent erupted when France won, 2–0. It was the same day the great Roger Federer lost at Wimbledon. Sports is an embarrassment of riches. And unlike the movies, it isn't scripted. It's for all of us to see when the magic happens, all over the world. It's why I've always hated the term "walk-off home run" for the double play—one of the most beautiful moments in baseball and sports as a whole. No one walks off—they celebrate, high-five, dance. "Walk-off" is so boring and among the stands I've taken, I've made it a point never to call it that.

One element of my career that I learned early, and so can you, is collaboration. No one landed on Normandy by himself. We need each other. What do we love about Tim Duncan or Bill Russell? Teamwork. It doesn't mean they weren't MVPs, the best at what they did. It means they were consistently able to be counted on, they were foundations of their teams. As Rudyard Kipling wrote, "The strength of the pack is the wolf, and the strength of the wolf is the pack." Perhaps this is why another element I haven't mastered well enough is to enjoy quiet and solitude. My husband does the *New York Times* crossword puzzle every morning and barely moves. There's much to be learned in closing out the noisy world.

It's okay to be courageous and honest, but it's also okay to take advice. Having lived my entire life as an outlier, I realize that being different is all right, too. Imagine being the first woman in hip-hop or on the Supreme Court. How difficult was that? Have no fear of being distinct, just try to have integrity when faced with a choice. I was offered a Miller Lite beer commercial thirty-five years ago, when the campaign was paying huge money and was enormously popular. The script called for me to pretend I was in a locker room. I had to pull a towel off a player, smile at the camera, and say, "*This* is all you have to know about locker room coverage." I said no thank you. They said I had no sense of humor. I never made jokes about the locker room. That was a place of business for me, not a cheap throwaway line. I never verbally crossed the sideline onto the playing field. That side is for the players; I am the reporter. I respect that the field is not my space nor my place. I took all the early abuse I had suffered—plenty of "What's *she* doing here?"—and I channeled it into humor. Yes, I've been embarrassed on occasion, humiliated on others (no one teaches a course in humiliation), but I hadn't been sold into marriage at sixteen or grown up under Taliban rule. I was covering sports! I learned to be confident in my abilities, and that made all the difference. I knew what I was looking at and I had the ability to translate it.

The legendary player Joe DiMaggio was once asked why he put his heart and soul into every at bat after playing for the Yankees for thirteen years. His answer was so simple and so profound: "Because," he said, "someone in the stands might be seeing Joe DiMaggio for the first time." I loved that thought and I want you to take it into every meeting, every greeting, every time you're on display. It might be the only time you interact with someone. The great Maya Angelou once wrote, "People will forget what you said, people will forget what you did, but people will never forget how you made them feel." Isn't that beautiful? Try it. It works. When I was a sophomore in college, I met Howard Cosell at the airport when he came to Boston for a Patriots game. I was leaving

With great announcer Howard Cosell in 1980

to visit a roommate and we ended up next to each other. I told him I aspired to work in sports. Many years later, I ran into Cosell in a press box, where he was both funny and rude. He said, "Open your coat," and I replied, "Take off your toupee." I couldn't believe my brain gave me that line that fast, but Cosell laughed and we went on to become friends. Toward the end of his life, we'd meet for lunch on Madison Avenue. He could only sip orange juice through a straw, but we enjoyed each other. It was how we made each other feel.

I was never interested in being famous—I wasn't even sure what it meant, unless it went with Dr. Jonas Salk or Martin Luther King Jr. I certainly wasn't going to rip people to get there. I wanted, in both print and TV, to be considered easy and original, even nostalgic if required. One time when Alberto Tomba, the skier, won the World Championship, I asked him how he was going to celebrate. He said, in his thick Italian accent, "I will follow you home." I quickly replied, "That's why they call you Al-Flirto Tomba."

I don't care if you're black or white or Hispanic, male or female, Catholic, Jewish, or Hindu; I had zero connections when I started—my father was from Nazi-occupied Holland and my mother was from a lower-middle-class Irish family that had never been out of New England. My mom always said, though, that I had "sand in my shoes," and that I was going somewhere. You can do the same. It's called desire, dedication, and focus. We can't all be Kareem Abdul-Jabbar, but we can all take one hundred skyhooks a day. We can't all be picked first on a team, but we can all show up to have a chance. Everything

Shakespeare didn't say, John Wooden or Red Auerbach did. Read what they wrote. Wooden's aphorisms were simple: "If you don't have the time to do it right, when will you have the time to do it over?" or "Never mistake activity for achievement." Red Auerbach had eleven principles for playoff basketball that he included in his book *Basketball for the Player, the Fan & the Coach*. They were not unlike Wooden's perfect pyramid for life—maybe a little rougher—but the ideas aren't that different. "The only correct actions are those that require no explanation and no apology," Auerbach wrote.

The Shakespeare play that had the most impact on me was the pastoral comedy *As You Like It*. There are themes of love and forgiveness, but the most important lesson in the play is risk. A group of people leave Duke Frederick's court, tired of the arbitrary justice, and take a chance on living with nothing in the Arden Forest. Such is life. You must take risks to learn about yourself, away from all that has made you comfortable. The late, great Christopher Hitchens once said, "DNA can tell you who you are, but not what you are." That is up to you. Think big, think small, but take a chance. And don't forget to write thank-you notes.

I've been blessed to have had a billion-dollar life, where I've been *paid* to go to London for Wimbledon or Shanghai for Yao Ming or France for the Olympics. I hope I've shared with you some of the lessons I learned, but anyone reading this can know one thing: It can happen to you.

With my husband Bob Kanuth at the 2013 CBS Christmas party in New York

ACKNOWLEDGMENTS

After more than forty years of covering sports, I have thousands and thousands of people to thank. First to those who really pushed me to do this, Tom and Jerry Caraccioli, Andrew Blauner, and my brother Chris. Bill Gladstone coached me through it and the people from BenBella Books, especially publisher Glenn Yeffeth, editor-in-chief Leah Wilson, and production editor Jessika Rieck have been terrific. A handful of men really gave me the chance to cover all these sports: Vince Doria, Dave Smith, Bill Griffith, Joe Concannon,and Tom Mulvoy from the *Boston Globe*; Ted Shaker, Neal Pilson, Peter Lund, Rob Correa, Les Moonves, and Sean McManus from CBS; plus Curt Gowdy Jr. and John Filippelli from my years at ABC. I always wanted to work for John Walsh and finally did at ESPN, and the *Globe* sports department is filled with people to thank: Dan Shaughnessy, Bud Collins, Peter Gammons, Bob Ryan, Kevin Dupont, John Powers, Leigh Montville, Ray Fitzgerald, Ron Borges, Alan Richman (who gave me a lock of Elvis Presley's hair), and especially the late Will McDonough. We had others who would join us at a bar in Faneuil Hall or in Kenmore Square: Judy Carlough, John Spooner, Mitch Sikora, Matt Storin, Suzanne and Bijette, Paul Szep, Rick and Joanne Pitino, Bob Rodophele, and

Tom Palmer (who bought me Van Morrison's *Astral Weeks* and took me on a flatbed Ford in western Kansas). Thanks to my BC roommates Jeanne and Lori and Joan (who let me play David Bowie's album fifty times in a row!), and my Brookline Village roommate, Jan. Can't forget Lou Bell and his bag of nothing, the Bruins' Nate Greenberg, or the late Boo Kleven.

It was the time of the early women sportswriters: Melissa Ludtke, Michele Himmelberg, Robin Herman, Lynne Snierson, Julie Ward, Tracy Dodds, Helene Elliot, Betti Cuniberti, Claire Smith, Nancy Cooney, and Susan Fornoff. Because of the size and prestige of the *Boston Globe*, I covered every game for a decade sitting between John Feinstein of the *Washington Post* and Dick Weiss of the *Philadelphia Daily News*, still great friends to this day. There are other national writers to be thanked—Curry Kirkpatrick, Mike Downey, Lenn Robbins, Tom Callahan, Dave Anderson, George Vescey, Ira Berkow, and especially Red Smith, who told me to "make a memory" every time I'd go someplace new. George Solomon, legendary editor of the *Washington Post* sports section, always rooted for women. The next generation of women sportswriters were equally talented: Sally Jenkins, Jill Lieber, Lisa Olson, Christine Brennan, Jackie MacMullan, Johnette Howard, Melissa Isaacson, Michelle Kaufman, Kristen Huckshorn, Linda Robinson, Judy Battista, and Alysse Minkoff. Because I was the only woman in the beginning, it took a while to gather the really close ones: Cindy Shmerler of *Tennis* magazine, Susan Kerr, Suzanne Smith, and LeslieAnne Wade from CBS. I love and thank the posse we had in New York for ten years, with a rotating cast of

Janice Platt, Cecily Lesko, Kim Bohuny, Jeane Willis, Barb Ricke, Jo Ann Ross, Chris Plonsky, Donna Orender, Amy Berg, Ann Liguori, Pat Hall, Tom Healy, Frank Vuono, and Joey C. We'd often finish the night at one of Tommy O'Neill's bars. Sometimes Suzanne Smith would have a "girls' night" at her apartment, along with Andrea Joyce, Robin Roberts, Cat Newman, Lydia Stephans, Alanna Campbell, Deb Gelman, Kathy Cook, Suzy Kolber, Marci Kempner, Mary Carillo, and the great Billie Jean King.

I thank Rick Majerus and Jim Valvano for being the funniest coaches and funniest people I ever met; both of them let me in their lives. Many coaches, athletes, and people in TV have been enormously helpful to me: the late Dean Smith, Coach K, Rollie Massimino,

With good friend Robin Roberts

Chuck Daly, Peter Gammage, Digger Phelps, Dr. Tom Davis, Gary Williams, Jerry Tarkanian, Roy Williams, Lou Carnesecca, Tom Izzo, Chris Mullin, Greg Anthony, Tommy Amaker, Jay Bilas, Dale Brown, Jack Hartman, Sam Jones, Joe Bertagna (who played goalie at Harvard and really was the goalie in *Love Story*), George Blaney, Mike Tirico, the entire Carlesimo family, Tom Coughlin, Steve Mariucci, Joe Gibbs, Denny Green, Marv Levy (who famously said before every game, "Where would you rather be than Right Here, Right Now?"), John Calipari, Slice, Doug Flutie, Terry Robiskie, Burt Bacharach, Paul Hornung, Lonnie Ali, Jerry Glanville, Jerry Richardson, Doris Burke, Jim Mandich, Tony LaRussa, Dick Stockton, Jim and Julie Boeheim, Rachel Nichols, Shelley Smith, Bonnie Bernstein, Anita Marks, Jemele Hill, Sage Steele, Betsy Ross, Beth Mowins, Trenni Kusnierek, Donna de Varona, Nancy Hogshead, Suzyn Waldman, Richard Johnson, Rusty Sullivan, Gene DeFilippo, Eddie Miller, Jack Grinold, Anita Collins, Ed Carpenter, Steve Nazro, Ronni Fisher, Suzanne Grande, Joel Drucker, Pam Ganley, Dick Friedman, Craig Miller, Suzy Shuster, Caton Bredar, Barry Weisbord, Glenn Mathis, Fran Labelle from NYRA, Tom Durkin, Carol and Michael Weisman, Sharon and Andy Chansen, John McClain, Pat Hanlon, Dereck Whittenburg, Joan Siegel, Pam and Sonny Vaccaro, Doris Burke, Bob Bache, Ed Goren, Ann O'Grady, Joe Bertagna, Ian Eagle, Ana Leaird, Jocelyn Kalsmith, Joellyn Lankin, Joe O'Donnell, Kelly Neal, Heather Albert, Susie and Tommy Penders, Max Visser, Beat Visser, Ellen Whalen, Ed Werder, Peter Rogan, Mike Pereira, Nick Faldo, Chris Berman, Al McGuire, Reid Oslin, Joel Drucker, Jim Otto,

Anthony Munoz, Junior Seau, Wendy Burch, George Schweitzer, Al Michaels, Dan Dierdorf, Dave Johnson, Tom Hammond and Charlsie Cantey, Mike Lupica, Lenny DeLuca, Faye DeHoff, Craig Silver, Lance Barrow, Dick Ebersol, Joe Valerio, Sandy Grossman, Bob Stenner, Lea Miller, Jim Tooley, Ray Stallone, Tom Odjakjian, who still loves the Big East, Dick Kelley, the former PR director for Boston College who died too young, Hank Goldberg, Larry Wahl, Joe Healey (and 305 East 50th St.), Sam Jones, Dave Goren, and the entire Pitino family, and of course, Vinnie, and Ralph Willard. Also thanks to Wayne Lukas, Ali and Shug McGaughey, Karl Schmitt, Steven Nagler, all the Bafferts, Jamie Saults, and Nick Zito for making the Triple Crown so much fun for six weeks straight.

Thanks to best friends Teri Schindler and Mike Gorman, Tom and Julie McGrath, Erin and Sean McDonough, Lorraine and Dick Vitale, Greg Gumbel, Ian Eagle, Terry Bradshaw, James Brown, Marcus Allen, Tom Shine, Eddie White, the Andruzzi family, Joe Iracane, Marty Aranoff, Bob Mansbach, Abby Lopez, Liz Dolan, Tony Segreto, Chris Sullivan, Mike Ornstein, Dick Enberg and Bill Walton, Don and Mary Anne Shula, the entire Lesko family, and Boomer and Cheryl Esiason. Thanks to Bryan in London and Timmy in Oslo, Josephine Traina at the Garden, and Jim Dunn in Boca. I was lucky to begin my TV career with Brent Musburger and Jim Nantz, Len DeLuca and Ric LaCivita, then added Shea Johnson, Janet O'Leary, Matty Hetzel, Deanna O'Toole, Peter Lund, John Madden, the Madden family, plus Madden Cruiser drivers Willie and Joe and Dave. Big thanks to Dan Marino, Bill Parcells, Jim Steeg, Tony Tortorici, Jay Wright, Jimmy

O'Brien, Gil Brandt, Mike Westhoff, Seth Davis, Gregg Popovich, Chris and Pat Riley, and producers David Blatt, Eric Mann, Lance Barrow, Charlie Bloom, Mike Horvath, George Veras, and Lindsey Felling. Bob Dekas and Bob Fishman had a huge impact on my career. All the people at both AWSM and WISE have been great. Thanks to Paul Doherty, former head of the English department at Boston College, and to David Barrett, who wrote my favorite song, "One Shining Moment" (and to Armen Keteyian, who brought it to CBS). Good friend Christian McBride has won half a dozen jazz Grammys, but he still loves that song as much as we do. Kisses to John Filo, Paula Breck,

With my great friend, five-time Grammy winner Christian McBride, who was Sting's bassist for fifteen years

Covering the NCAA tournament with broadcast partners Bill Raftery and Verne Lundquist

and the entire CBS photo department. As always, to all my cousins, plus David and Amy Kanuth and baby Brady.

The NBA was fun with Pat O'Brien, and I got to travel the world with Peggy Fleming, Dick Button, Brian Boitano, Terry Gannon, and legendary skating director Doug Wilson. My March Madness partners, Verne Lundquist and Bill Raftery, are two of the most entertaining people on the planet, along with producer Mark Wolff. Thanks to Barry Frank and Sandy Montag, who've been with me for thirty years, and equal thanks to American Sportscasters Association president Lou Schwartz, who's been watching over our industry for four decades. I was blessed to cover games with Frank Gifford, go horseback riding with Emmitt Smith, go bowling with Jerome Bettis, and go to a carnival with Wesley Walls. I listened to Chris Doleman play the saxophone by moonlight and golfed badly with Marshall Faulk. I once went to an art gallery with Curtis Martin. Producer Ritchie Zyontz and director Artie Kempner let me keep my luggage in the FOX truck when CBS sent me to one of their NFC playoff games. I thank them, for that and for the hot chocolate, too. Thanks to Tom Ryan, former CEO of CVS, for being a blast at the Final Four. Extra thanks to the Buonicontis, for fighting the fight, and to Dr. Barth Green and the Safie family for helping everywhere they can.

New York Giants founder Wellington Mara had a Mass said for me when I shattered my hip in Central Park in

In Ireland with Dan Rooney, late owner of the Pittsburgh Steelers

With legendary coach of the Dallas Cowboys, Jimmy Johnson

the early 1990s—his son John, the gentleman son of a gentleman and now president of the Giants, lived next door to me at Boston College. I have appreciation for Joe Gibbs, Al Davis, Denny Green, Tom Coughlin, Mike Holmgren, Andy Reid, Lovie Smith, and Tony Dungy, the "Chief" Art Rooney and his late son Dan—plus Lawrence Taylor, Reggie White, Steve Young, Jim McMahon, Harry Carson, and Brett Favre for being especially kind when it mattered. And thanks to Jimmy Johnson, Jason Taylor, Troy Aikman, Michael Irvin, Emmitt Smith, Charles Haley, Nate Newton, Big E, and the Jerry Jones family for being so great to me when they ruled the league. Also to Rudy Martzke, Larry Stewart, Dusty Saunders, Steve Lapa, Tom Hoffarth, Len Shapiro, Chad Finn, and John

Ourand for noticing my work. Thanks to the women who are so good at their jobs, Kim Jones, Pam Oliver, and Michele Tafoya. My deepest thanks to Patriots owner Robert Kraft and Hall of Famer Eddie DeBartolo, both whom I first interviewed in 1976.

There are plenty of radio people to thank for always having me on, beginning with those three fools on stools in Miami—Jeff DeForrest, Paulie-Man, and Dave Gergely, and thanks to their producer Mike Lubitz. Tony Kornheiser and Mike Wilbon have always been smart and funny, as are South Florida giants Footy, Mike Marino, and Hank Goldberg. Mike Francesa always treated me like the little sister he had to take to the park, but still put me on. The WEEI guys from Boston are wonderful, as are Kelly Whiteside, Mike Freeman, and Dave Goren. Suzyn Waldman has been a friend for decades, as have Andrea Kremer and Amy Trask. David Berson, Tyler Hale, Harold Bryant, and Emilie Deutsch came up with the idea for an all-female network sports talk show, produced by Julie Keryc and Amy Samalson. *We Need To Talk* has some of the greatest talent, including Tracy Wolfson, Swin Cash, Lisa Leslie, and Allie LaForce. Dana Jacobson and Katrina Adams are gems. Don't test Laila Ali about boxing or go swimming with either Dara Torres or Summer Sanders. If you haven't heard "The Fabulous Sports Babe" in Tampa, you should find her, and she's been much nicer to me than Don Imus, who once wrote me a letter that said, "Lesley, this is to officially inform you I am no longer in love with you; in fact, you bore me."

After three hip replacements and two spine operations, I've earned the broken bones I've acquired running everywhere from Lyon, France, to the hills of San Francisco, to the well-worn paths of Hyde Park in London, to the flat beaches in Florida. Doctors Nicholas, Cohen, Garami, Wittels, Callari, Brissett, Garcia, and Kannell and their staffs, especially Elizabeth, Ralph, Bettina, Naomi, Carmen, and Mal McHugh, have made me practically whole and ready to tackle the next assignment. Many thanks to them. I also thank every public relations guy (they were all guys back then) who took my calls and didn't tell me to go away, especially Jeff Blumb, Rich Dalyrmple, Scott Berchtold, Roger Valdisierri, Pat Hanlon, Stacey James, Kevin Byrne, Dan Edwards, Bill Keenist, Jim Saccomano, Kenny Klein, Frank Ramos, Kirk Reynolds, Chad Steele, and Ed Croke. And thanks to all the cameramen for being so patient, especially Dave A. and Andy K.

I owe a great debt to the league commissioners, particularly when they hadn't seen a woman around press row before. Pete Rozelle and David Stern opened the locker rooms, and were followed by equally great men, Paul Tagliabue and Adam Silver. Greg Aiello was wonderful throughout the many years, and thanks to Roger Goodell. Dave Gavitt at the Big East was decades ahead of his time, and the next commissioner, Mike Tranghese, was just as honorable. Also deserved thanks to Dave Baker, Steve Schott, and all the people at the Pro Football Hall of Fame. Thanks to NYU's Arthur Miller, Art Kaplan, Bob Costas, and the social work we're trying to do. And the same to the Muhammad Ali Foundation in Louisville, which is trying to spread his generous principles of life. Two charities have had an enormous impact on me:

St. Jude's, helped by Cheryl DeLeonardis, Kaye Burkhardt, and Cheri and Pat Summerall; and the V Foundation for Cancer Research, now led by George Bodenheimer, Steve Bornstein, Pam Valvano, and Susan Braun. As a board member for more than twenty years, I have thanked Bobby Lloyd, Pam Valvano, John Leshney, Harry Rhoads, Geoff Mason, Larry Probst, Becky Bumgardner, Julie and Jim Allegro, Mike McDonald, Bob Valvano, Rosa Gatti, and the brilliant doctors many, many times.

Now living in Florida, I get to hang with my husband Bob, whom I thank every day, along with pals Jersey Kyle, Connie Coopersmith, Fudge Browne, Mary Fanizzi,

With former CEO of ESPN and fellow board member of the V Foundation for Cancer Research George Bodenheimer

Jennifer, Judith, Jennifer Kronenberg, Jelitza Ortiz, Mike and Alice, Dan and Grace, Judith, Carolyn and Adam Hasid, Charlie Brown, Mike and Alicia Piazza, Pete Sandore, Mike Gdovic, Sean Reilly, Eddie, Lori, and Bradley Saltzman, Carl, the Sultan, Sardy and Foxy, the Bruders, Billy and Christie Evans, Jack Shelley, Harvey and Cathy Greene, the Bistro and Emilios, especially JC, Emily Peterson, Ferdie, Mustang Sally, Bob Farmer and Tommy Winston, Steve Alaimo, Michael and Kathleen O'Neil, Doc Pratt, Haresh and Tanuja, Mike Shehadi and his talented daughter Lauren, Mike Mailey, Dopey O'Donnell, Judy Dalail, Jack Freedman, and Billy Campbell—all of whom make living in Miami a blast.

And not to be forgotten over the many miles and smiles (and a few tears at night) are a few more friends and colleagues: Gayle Barden, Peg Carson, the secretary who kept the *Globe* sports department together, the late Dick Bresciani of the Red Sox, and Mike Shalin, still writing after all these years. My deep thanks go to Robin Brendle, Dan Sabreen, and especially Jen Sabatelle of the CBS communications department, and always to Rick and Janet Odioso, who make every year on Radio Row at the Super Bowl another long day to remember. And also to lifelong friends Kris Kellem and Tom Jernstedt of CBS and the NCAA. I have appreciation for the people who cover our business, Ken Fang, Neil Best, Barry Jackson, Chad Finn, Richard Deitsch, and Phil Mushnick (who, every time he criticized me was right), and I miss calling people like Lee Remmel of the Packers, Ron Howard and Derek Boyko of the Eagles, Brett Daniels of the Cowboys,

Craig Kelley of the Colts, and even crazy Al LoCasale of the Raiders. Certainly, I don't want to forget thanking Gary Wright, my two Charlies—Taylor and Dayton—and, of course, Rick Smith of the Rams. A special hug to the fans, without whom none of us would have jobs! Red Roses to all.

ABOUT THE AUTHOR

Lesley Visser is the most highly acclaimed female sportscaster of all time. She is the first and only woman in the Pro Football Hall of Fame; the only female sportscaster to have carried the Olympic torch; the only woman to have presented the championship Lombardi Trophy at the Super Bowl; and the first woman on the network broadcasts of the Final Four, the Super Bowl, the NBA Finals, and the World Series. She was voted the Outstanding Female Sportscaster of All Time by the National Sportscasting Association, was also elected to the Sportswriters Hall of Fame for her work at the *Boston Globe*, national magazines, and CBS.com, and was recently elected to the Sports Broadcasting Hall of Fame. Visser was the first and only woman to win the Billie Jean King Outstanding Journalist award, was named a *Sports Business Journal* Champion, and was also elected to the Sports Museum of Boston. A graduate of Boston College, which awarded her an honorary doctorate in 2007, she has been on the board of the V Foundation for Cancer Research for more than twenty years, while also serving on the board of NYU's Sports and Society. Visser has mentored young women for decades, while speaking at colleges and businesses around the world.

A sportscaster at CBS for more than twenty-five years, she also spent nearly ten years at ABC sports, where she became the first woman on *Monday Night Football*, while also covering the World Series, World Figure Skating, the World Skiing Championships, and the Triple Crown. She has been voted one of the "Women We Love" by *Esquire* magazine and one of the "Five Ideal Dinner Guests" by *GQ*. Most recently, she was honored by the Muhammad Ali Center as a "Daughter of Greatness," in recognition of her leadership and dedication to activism and pursuit of justice. She and her husband, Bob Kanuth, a former captain of Harvard basketball, live in Bay Harbor Islands, Florida.